I G. Collecott
1985.

JAPANESE BRUSH PAINTING

JAPANESE BRUSH PAINTING

The Art of Sumi Painting

Takahiko Mikami

DAVID & CHARLES
NEWTON ABBOT LONDON

First published in Japan by Shufunotomo Co., Ltd.
6, Kanda Surugadai 1-chome, Chiyoda-ku, Tokyo, 101 Japan

First published in the United Kingdom in 1985 by
David & Charles (Publishers) Limited
Brunel House Newton Abbot Devon

Printed in Japan

Contents

Foreword

I was born in Tokyo, Japan in 1916 and started painting when I was nine years old. I studied painting both in Tokyo and in New York, and lived in San Francisco, California for thirteen years.

In 1957 I established the Japanese Art Center School of Fine Arts in San Francisco, where I taught Sumi Painting which I popularized as "Japanese Brush Painting." I also gave instruction in this art over the National Educational Television Network (NET) in the United States through KQED in San Francisco, and thanks to the video-taping of several series, my instruction continued well over my thirteen-year residence. The tapes also traveled outside of the United States to various countries, such as New Zealand, from which I would receive mail from my "students" informing me so. I understand that I "spoke perfect Portuguese" in Brazil!

I also had the opportunity to teach Sumi Painting in Europe through the television series produced by the Bertelsmann Fernseh Produktion in Munich, West Germany.

I have published eight books on Sumi Painting, seven of which are written in English. This book is intended for anyone anywhere who is interested in Sumi Painting, whether or not he has tried it before or even held a paint brush previously. I have included a variety of painting subjects which I believe would be of interest to non-Japanese.

There are many books on Sumi Painting published in English, but I believe that this type of book should not be merely a translation of a book for the Japanese people into English. All books for the Japanese are, of course, understood easily by the Japanese, but the contents are not always easy for foreigners to understand. This is not just because of the difference in culture or the unfamiliar words or unusual tools. For instance, the shapes and sizes of trees, flowers, vegetables, etc.

in Japan are very often different from those in other countries. So, in order to teach these subjects to those outside of Japan, it is desirable to stay in these foreign countries for a fairly long period, first of all, to understand the daily lives and customs of the people living there, also the differences in the ways of thinking. Fortunately, my long residence in the United States and frequent visits to other countries help me greatly in this respect.

Suppose I paint a Japanese eggplant and show it to an American. He might not think that it is an eggplant as the size and shape of the vegetable in the United States is quite different.

I have painted a persimmon to have many Caucasians (never having seen the fruit) exclaim, "Ah, a tomato!"

In English something can be described as 'straight as a pine.' However, the Japanese pine tree is often found growing at an angle or rather crooked in shape—naturally weathered by the wind or intentionally formed at the hands of the Japanese gardener.

These seemingly little differences, however, are actually not so little, for in studying traditional Sumi Painting, many of the subjects are also traditional and used to teach certain strokes. For someone who had never actually seen what he was painting, whether it was a single object or a landscape, this could present a few problems. I have taken these differences into consideration, as much as possible, in writing this book. True, I cannot eliminate certain subjects which are essential to this art, but I have added a number of non-traditional subjects as examples of how you can adapt what you have learned to paint subjects you are more familiar with.

This book is about the particular style of painting called Sumi Painting or *sumi-e* (soo mee ay); *sumi*=black ink, *e*=

picture. Basically, Sumi Painting uses black ink only but is also painted with some colors and is then called *tansai sumi-e*; *tansai*=lightly-colored. Whether in black ink only or otherwise, *sumi-e* is painted in simple strokes and dots, and once a stroke is made you should not go over it again. Any corrections can be detected—you cannot fool *sumi* ink. The different tones and various effects of the strokes, together with the handling of space (which I call negative space), are appreciated in this painting of simplicity. Only what is necessary is painted. The presence of something may be suggested without its form actually visible in the painting . . . and yet it is definitely there. This is a study in the economy of strokes. The portion that is left unpainted is just as important as the painted area. Although this type of painting may seem foreign to you, I find that knowing it can be extremely helpful in any other medium, whether it be oils or watercolors or otherwise. Many of my non-Japanese students also share my opinion. Gaining control of the brush is the main reason.

Through this book I hope many readers outside of Japan will become interested in trying their hand at *sumi-e*, and in doing so learn to appreciate the beauty of simplicity as interpreted in this style of painting.

May I wish you "Good painting!"

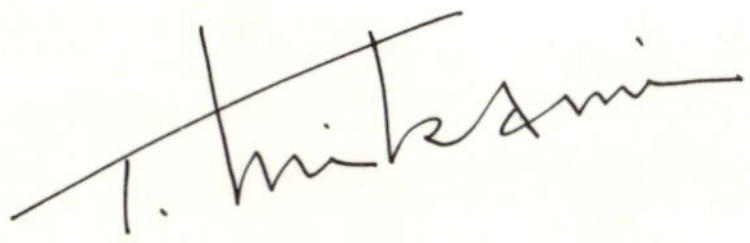

TAKAHIKO MIKAMI

Introduction

Sumi Painting is based on simple lines and dots in black *sumi* ink, or sometimes black ink strokes with some colors.

This particular style of painting should be done using a Japanese or Chinese brush with bamboo holder, preferably on handmade Japanese paper or painting silk, and not on slippery, non-absorbent, machine-made paper. (Easily acquired substitutes for Japanese paper are given later in the book.)

The techniques of Sumi Painting are centuries old and have been handed down from one Japanese master to another. The characteristic of this painting style is in how to express what is in the painter's mind in a few simple strokes without the use of many colors other than the black.

Japanese art had its beginning more than fourteen hundred years ago as a result of the introduction of Buddhism to Japan from the Asian Continent. It then developed along with Buddhism as the religion spread its roots throughout the country, although not always at a steady pace. Meanwhile, nature following its set course, quietly surrounded the artist with its seasonal changes, always ready to become the subject of a painting. As only religious subjects were painted at first, it was mainly the priests who undertook this task, i.e. the priests were the artists of the time. However, gradually the artists came to observe and paint subjects of nature more and more, rather than confining themselves to religious themes only, despite the fact that it was the influence of Buddhism which actually promoted the development of this art at its start. To explain the art and its connection with Zen Buddhism would take up another book in itself. In present day Japan, *sumi-e* in general is no longer thought of as representing the religion (although as a background the Buddhist theory cannot be ignored), and is the highly stylized art now appreciated internationally.

This book is not intended to be a strict art course. I have tried to simplify the presentation and make it easy to understand. This is a book intended for your enjoyment.

Anyone can enjoy painting in this style—you don't necessarily need talent. All you need is practice!

Equipment

Sumi Painting is the art of utmost simplicity, not only in artistic expression but in the equipment it calls for. In comparison with other painting techniques Sumi Painting needs only a few tools which are very simple, but should be the right ones.

In the old days in Japan, artists were proud of possessing and using expensive equipment, because they thought that expensive tools were a great help to their technique. This way of thinking is sometimes correct if the tools match the technique of the artists. It is something like expensive golf clubs for good golfers. The same thing can be said of Sumi Painting. My advice is to have the right tools to suit the user. Just remember that expensive equipment does not necessarily make good painters.

SUMI (ink)

The *sumi* ink stick is usually rectangular in shape and about the size of a finger. There are variations in size, shape and quality. It is made up mainly of carbon and glue. *Sumi* has long been used for writing and painting both in Japan and China. The ink stick usually has some lettering on it showing the trade name it goes by and the name of the manufacturer.

Aged *sumi* is supposed to be good, but old *sumi* sticks crack very easily, especially with present day heating and air conditioning, and in countries with dry climates.

The *sumi* ink stick does not produce ink by itself. It is used together with the *suzuri* ink stone. You need water on the surface of the *suzuri* on which you rub the *sumi* stick to make black ink. Although *sumi* is mostly black, there are a few exceptions such as red *sumi* which is usually used by the master or teacher to correct the mistakes of his pupils.

As for black *sumi* ink, some have brownish tints, some bluish, the latter usually used in Sumi Painting.

BOKUJŪ (liquid *sumi* ink)

Liquid *sumi* ink is a fairly modern product in Japan and comes in a tube, bottle or can. To use this kind of ink for traditional *sumi-e* is contrary to the traditional way of thinking. But there is no reason why we should not utilize it to produce traditional art, especially in this day and age, if the situation at hand proves it to be more convenient. This will save you the time and effort to make ink on the *suzuri*, although you should practice and know how to make ink yourself and get used to using both. You will find it convenient knowing how to use both self-made and ready-made ink. The *bokujū* comes in both ready-to-use and concentrate consistency, the latter having to be diluted accordingly.

SUZURI (ink stone)

The *suzuri* is the afore-mentioned ink-rubbing stone. It is black and carved out of a slate-like rock, the usual shape being rectangular. It comes in different sizes, a medium sized one about 3 by 5 inches and about ½ inch thick (approx. 7.5 cm. × 12.5 cm. × 1.25 cm.) being sufficient for ordinary use. Surrounded by a shallow rim on three sides is the flat portion on which ink is made by rubbing the *sumi* ink stick with water. This flat rubbing surface called 'the land,' slopes down at the other end to form a deep portion or ink-well called 'the sea.' The 'sea' end should always be placed away from you. First pour some water into the ink-well and holding your ink vertically with the flat end down, draw up some water to 'the land.' Rub your *sumi* stick with the water to make your ink, rubbing back and forth or in a circular motion. Pick up ink from 'the land' with your brush. From time to time water is replenished from the well as needed and the ink stick rubbed accordingly, as the ink on your *suzuri* should always be kept a dark black. After each use the *suzuri* should be emptied and rinsed off of excess ink.

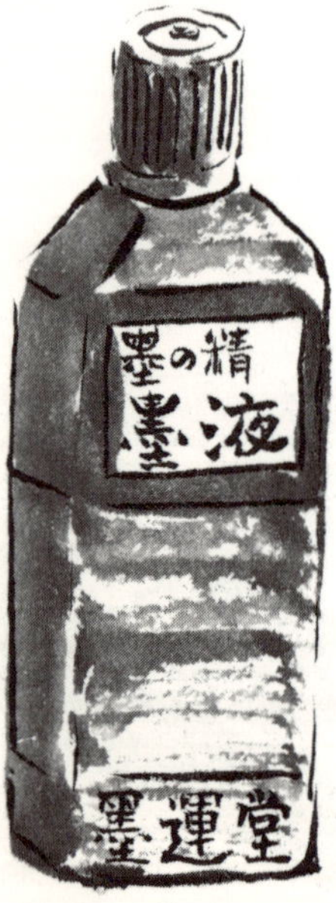

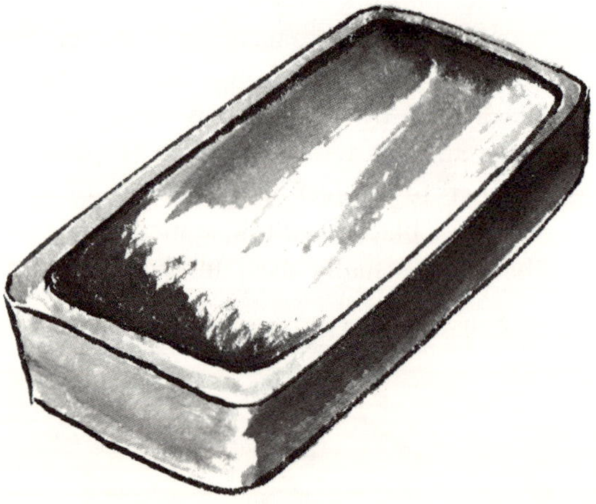

FUDE (brush)

Fude (foo day) means brush for both painting and writing, and when I mention a *fude* brush in this book I, of course, mean a painting brush which is similar in appearance to a writing brush but made differently. Usually a *fude* brush for painting has a slightly longer bamboo holder than that of a writing brush.

A *fude* brush is made with the hair of the deer, badger, sheep or other animals.

The head of a new brush is usually protected by a plastic cap. This cap should be thrown away once the brush has been put to use. Do not try to fit it onto the used brush again.

Before using a stiff new brush, rinse it out first in cold water to soften the head, pressing it out a few times. This will dissolve the paste holding the hairs together. Never use hot water with your brush as it will loosen the hairs. Take good care of your brushes being sure to wash them after each use. You may wash your painting brush as many times as you wish, but with some writing brushes the bristles may loosen and drop out of the holder when handled in the same way.

A *fude* brush should have a sharply pointed tip and the bristles should be flexible. For the beginner, a *tsuketate* (tsoo kay tah tay) brush is suitable.

The *fude* is held between thumb and forefinger or thumb and middle finger, and is usually kept perpendicular to the painting surface. The position of the fingers on the brush depends on what is being painted. The following illustrations will help you to paint in the correct way.

(1) In most cases hold the brush straight up to draw lines and stokes, except for shaded strokes and wide dry-brush strokes.
(2) Hold the upper part of the holder when painting large strokes.
(3) Hold the middle part of the holder when painting medium size strokes.
(4) Hold the lower part of the holder for detailed work. You may let your little finger steady your hand by keeping it on the paper surface.

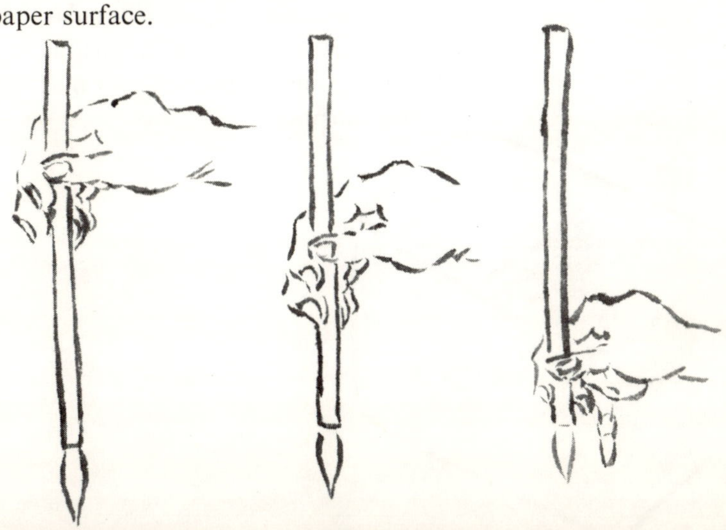

PAPER ● ***WASHI* paper** *Sumi* painting is usually done on what Westerners call rice paper and what we call *washi* in Japan. (Actually, there is no such thing as 'rice paper' in Japan.) The name *washi* means Japanese handmade paper in contrast with Western machine-made paper. There are many different types of handmade paper in Japan, but *gasenshi* and *tōshi* are two of the most popular among *sumi-e* artists.

● ***SHIKISHI* paper board** The *shikishi* is made with handmade paper such as *gasenshi*, *torinoko*, gold or silver paper mounted on cardboard. Of these, I recommend *gasenshi* for *sumi* painting. The *shikishi* is rectangular in shape and comes in several standard sizes, the usual one used for *sumi-e* measuring 9½ by 10¾ inches (24.3 cm × 27.3 cm).

● **Illustration board** When I was living in San Francisco, I found illustration board suitable for painting *sumi-e* when Japanese paper was not always available. Illustration board is white paper mounted on thick cardboard.

● **Newsprint** Newsprint (unprinted newspaper) is inexpensive paper that can be found in any country and is good for practicing *sumi* painting. You can also practice on old newspapers.

● ***EGINU* silk** *Sumi-e* is also painted on *eginu* (ay gee noo) silk which means silk for painting. It is usually sized to make painting on it easy. When using *eginu* for painting, you must stretch it first on a frame similar to stretching canvas for oil painting.

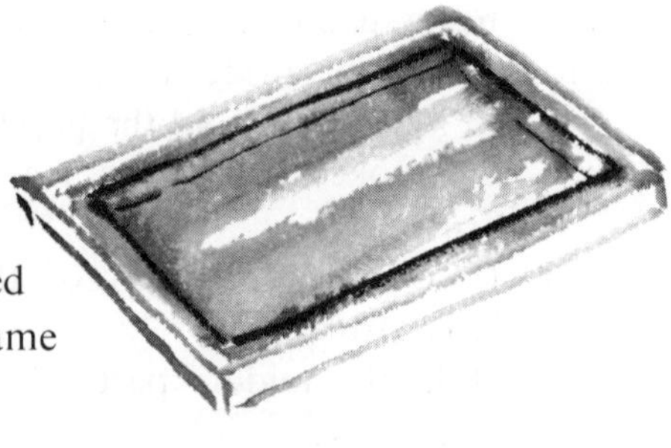

Edges pasted onto frame

***FUDE-ARAI* (water well)** The *fude-arai* is the water well that holds water for washing out the brush, also for thinning *sumi* ink on the brush. Those sold commercially are circular or rectangular in shape with compartments, come in various sizes, and are usually made of white china. However, you may use any deep bowl or cup for this purpose.

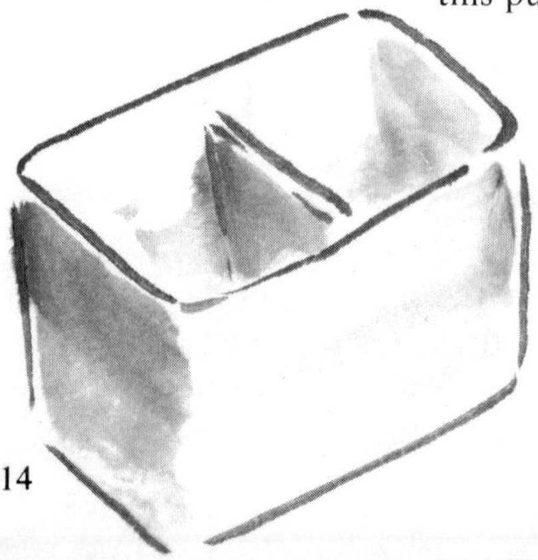

The *sara* is a small white dish which is used as a palette for testing the color of ink or for thinning the ink for different tones. Although sold commercially in plain and fancy shapes and various sizes, any dish, preferably white, is fine. You will find a saucer good for this purpose.

SARA
(dish)

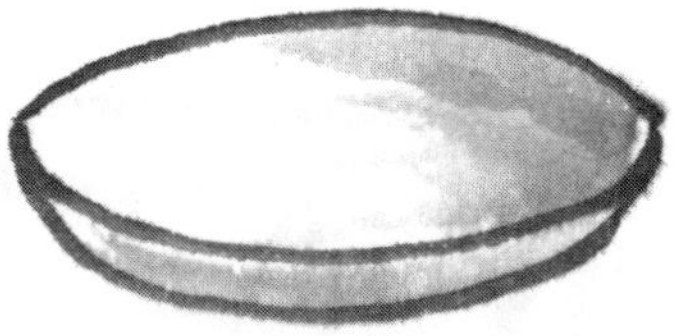

The *fude-fuki* or brush wiper is absorbent cotton material used to soak up excess water on the brush or to wipe the brush on. Old towels are fine. Large pieces should be cut to convenient size and folded into "a pad." When you do not have appropriate material on hand, you may use facial tissues for a substitute.

FUDE-FUKI
(cloth)

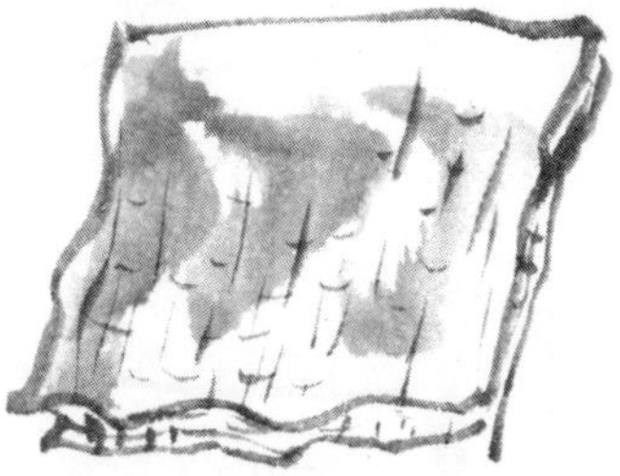

When you paint on paper, place the *bunchin* weight near the top edge so that the paper will not move while painting. Anything heavy will do. Even a fairly large stone wrapped in paper is sufficient, the latter to cover any rough surfaces or sharp edges. Commercially made *bunchin* come in various shapes and sizes, some quite artistic. Narrow rectangular shapes are very common.

BUNCHIN
(paper weight)

A sheet of felt or flannel should be placed under the painting paper so that any excess moisture will be absorbed.

MŌSEN
(felt)

As mentioned previously, basically *sumi* painting is done in black *sumi* ink only but watercolors are often used together with *sumi* brush strokes, at which time it is called *tansai sumi* painting. For instance, flower petals can be painted in color and all other parts with black *sumi* ink. This kind of painting is the *tansai sumi-e.*

ENOGU
(watercolors)

Although there are typical Japanese watercolors for Japanese-style paintings, you may use any watercolor which is used for Western-style watercolor painting. Either colors in tubes or in cake-form are fine. Japanese watercolors do have some shades which differ slightly in tone and which you may be tempted to call something like 'persimmon red' or 'oriental blue.'

Position of Equipment

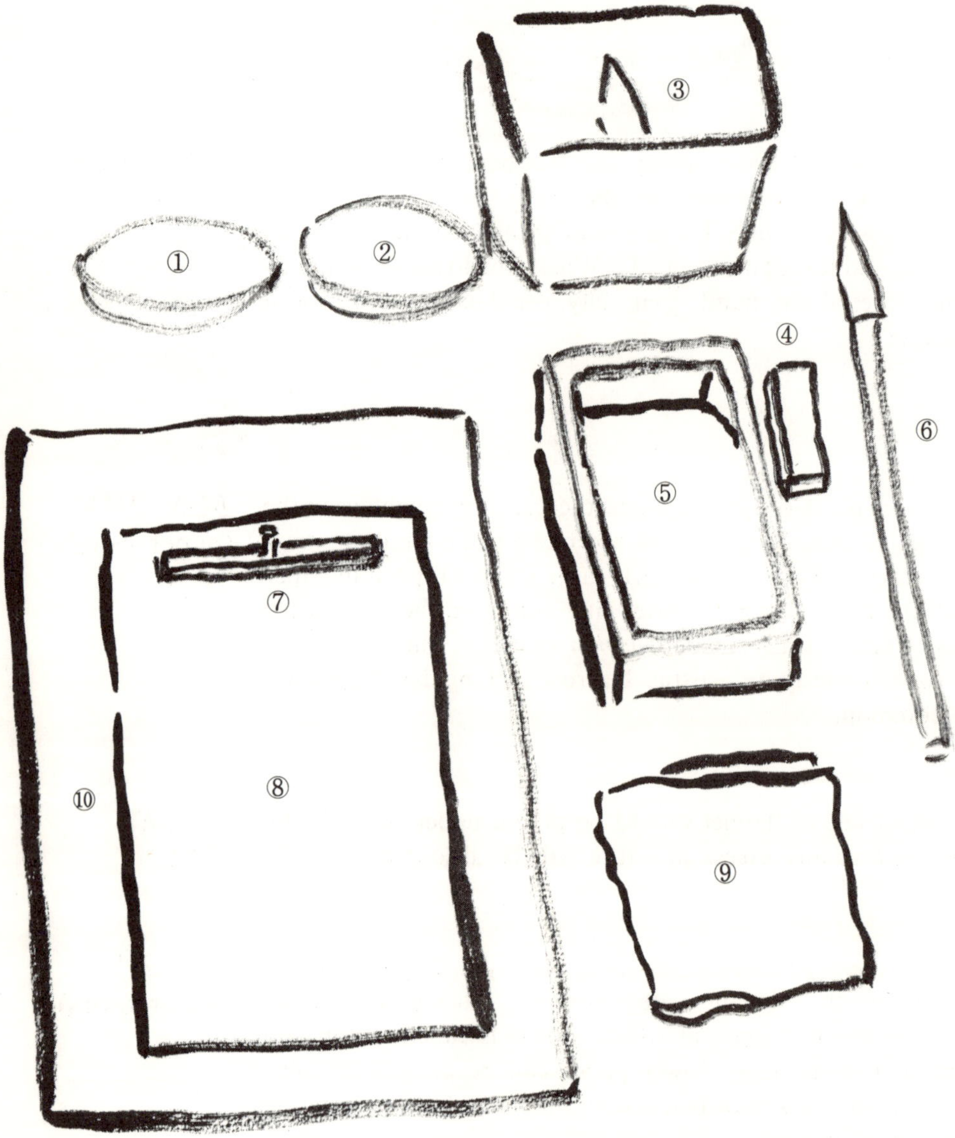

① *Sara*
② *Sara*
③ *Fude-arai*
④ *Sumi*
⑤ *Suzuri*
⑥ *Fude*
⑦ *Bunchin*
⑧ *Paper*
⑨ *Fude-fuki*
⑩ *Mōsen*

Left-handers may reverse the positions.

Basic Painting Techniques

Lesson 1 - *Unpitsu*

● How to control your brush

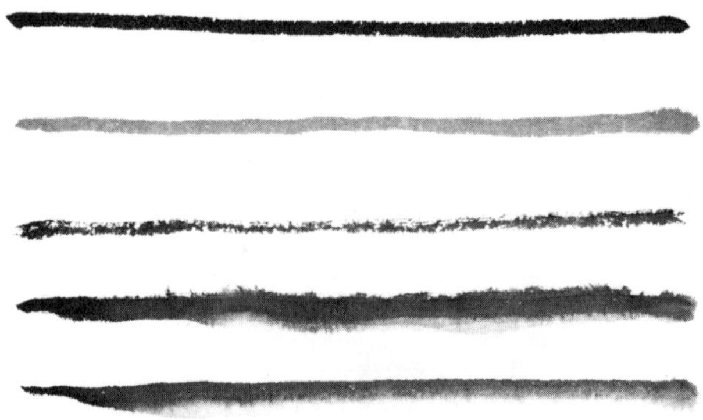

(1) Dark color

(2) Light color

(3) *KASURE*

(4) *NIJIMI*

(5) *BOKASHI*

All of the preceding lines were painted by holding the brush straight up, painting from left to right. If left-handed, you may of course reverse the order and paint from right to left. (The following numbers coincide with those above.)

(1) Use dark color ink.

(2) Pick up dark color ink on the tip of your brush and transfer it onto a dish. Add some water to it with your brush to make light color ink.

(3) Make medium color ink by adding a little bit of water to dark ink on your dish. Pick up the medium color ink with the tip of your brush, wiping off the excess ink on your *fude-fuki* cloth. Use this dry brush to draw the *KASURE* (kah soo ray) line.

(4) Dip your brush into the water, take off some of the excess water on your *fude-fuki* cloth and pick up dark color ink. Use this wet brush to draw the *NIJIMI* (nee jee mee) line.

(5) Wash your brush with water. Wipe off excess water on your *fude-fuki* and pick up dark color ink only at the tip of your brush. Remember, black ink is **only at the tip**. Draw the *BOKASHI* shaded line from left to right.

After practicing these lines horizontally, continue practicing them vertically from top to bottom. Remember that between the dark and light tones, the grades of color are actually infinite.

Lesson 2 - *Bokashi*

● The shaded stroke

In Lesson 1 you learned that with just one touch of your brush, you could draw a shaded line showing both dark and light tones. Let us study shading a bit further.

First, wash your brush with clean water, lightly patting off the excess water on your *fude-fuki*. Your brush, of course, contains only water at this point. Next, add light color ink to half of your brush, then pick up dark color ink on the tip.

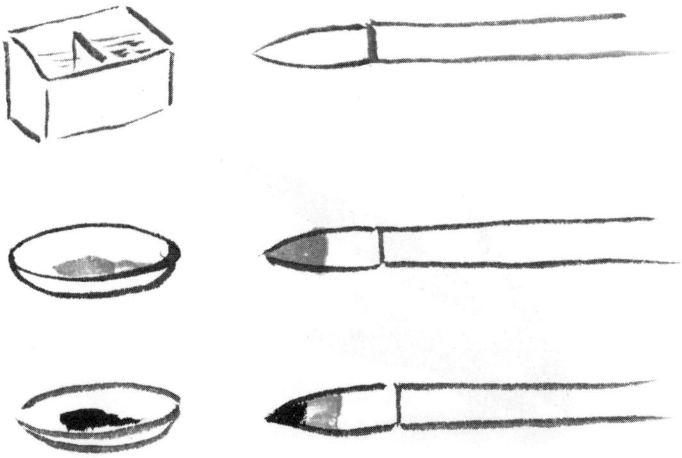

Only water

Light color ink

Dark ink on the tip

Hold the brush slanted or almost flat against the paper, and draw straight or curved strokes.

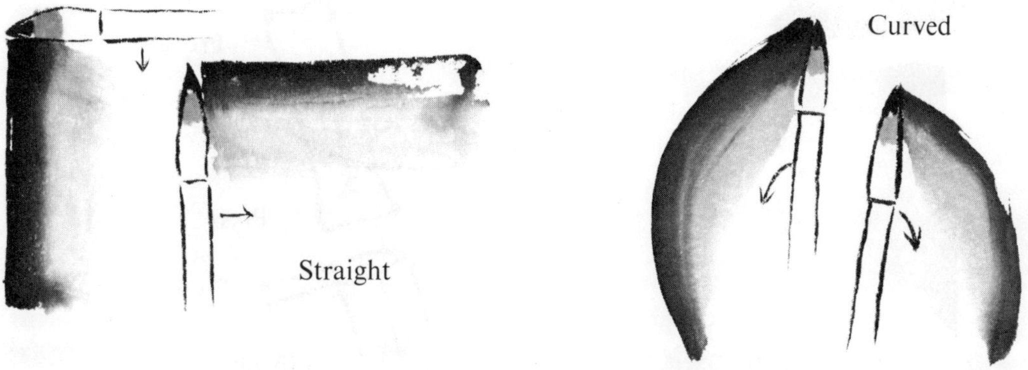

First—light color ink

Next—pick up dark color

(1) Apply light color ink to the entire brush.
(2) Pick up dark color ink at the tip.
(3) Use the brush slanted or almost flat against the paper painting from bottom to top for the bamboo trunk. (Bamboo will be explained in detail on pages 26–35.)

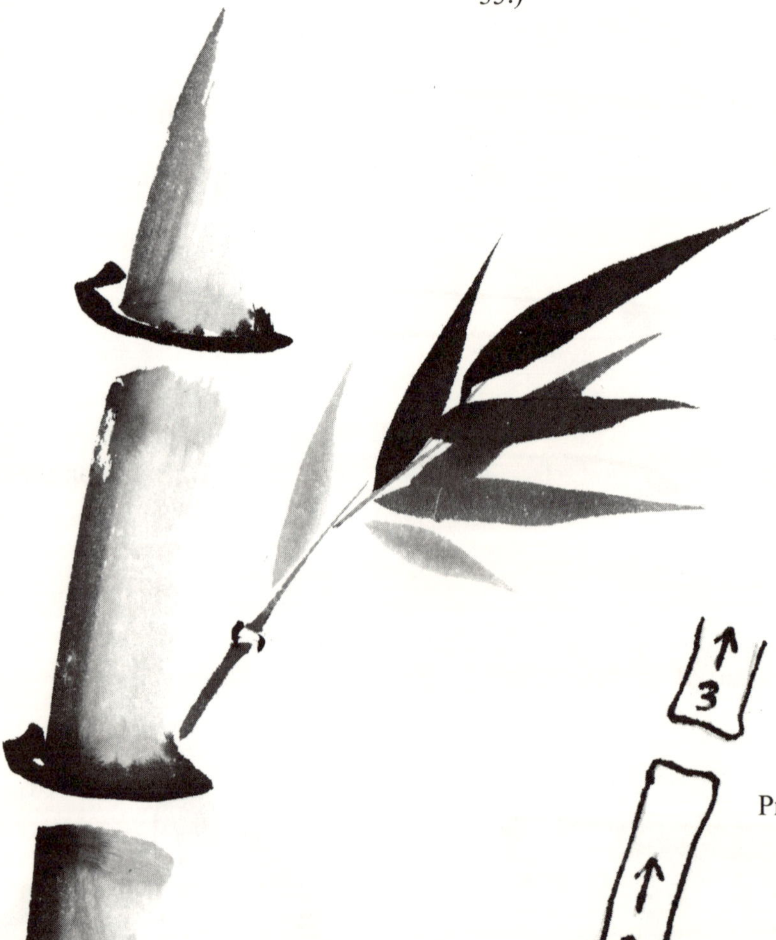

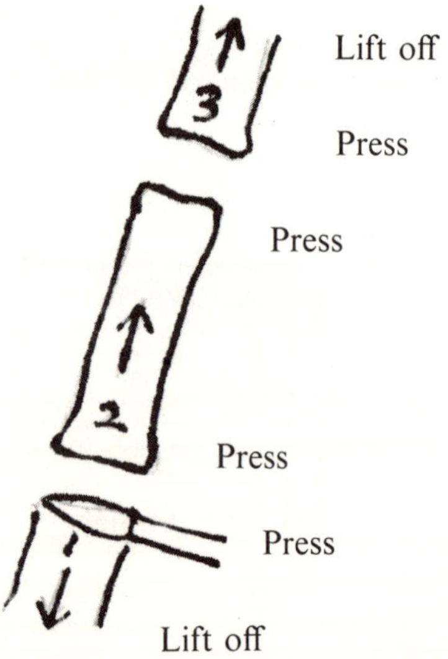

Lesson 3 - *Men-gaki*

● How to fill in flat areas such as the sky

Using your brush flat or slanted, draw a wide stroke with the same speed from the beginning to the end. Repeat this stroke immediately alongside the previous one. Do not wait long in between, otherwise the moisture from both strokes will not spread out and join, making two separate strokes instead.

Try not to overlap the second stroke too much as it will make a very dark portion.

Keep adding as many strokes as necessary depending on the size of the area you wish to fill in.

Lesson 4 - *Nō-tan*

● Darkness and lightness: contrast in tone

Nō means dark, and *tan* light. A *sumi* painting consists of a variety of *nō* and *tan*. For example, even a single tree leaf looks artistic when it shows both *nō* and *tan*.

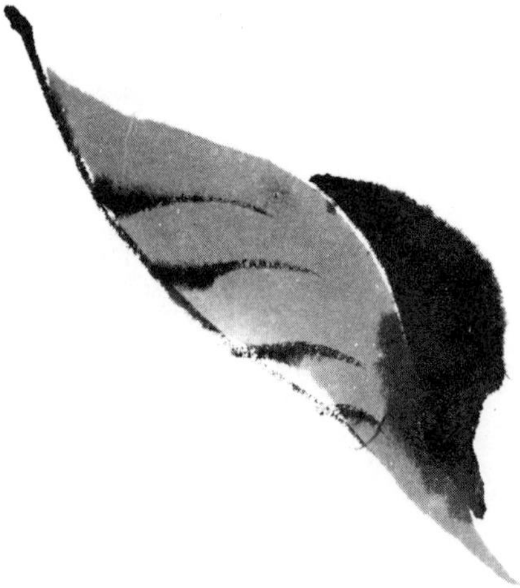

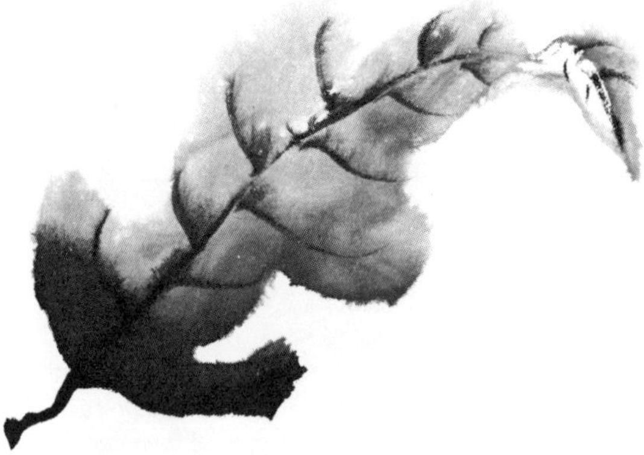

In just one stroke you can show *nō-tan* using the shaded stroke.

You can also produce *nō-tan* by adding dark color ink over light or medium color ink strokes. In this case, add dark color ink immediately after the light or medium color stroke is drawn while it is still wet. Otherwise, the dark color will stand out by itself, not blending in with the lighter tone.

Light color

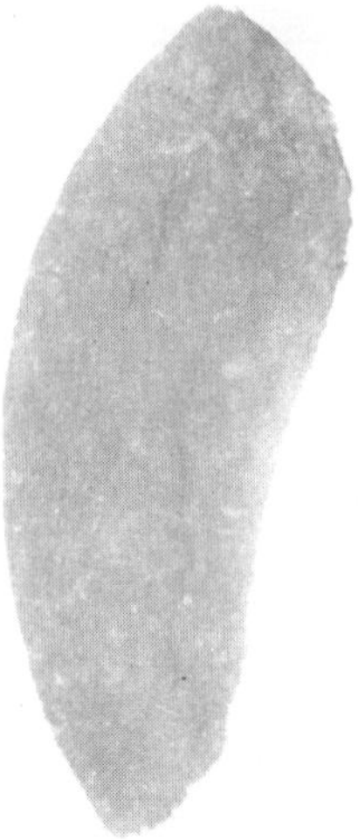

Dark ink added

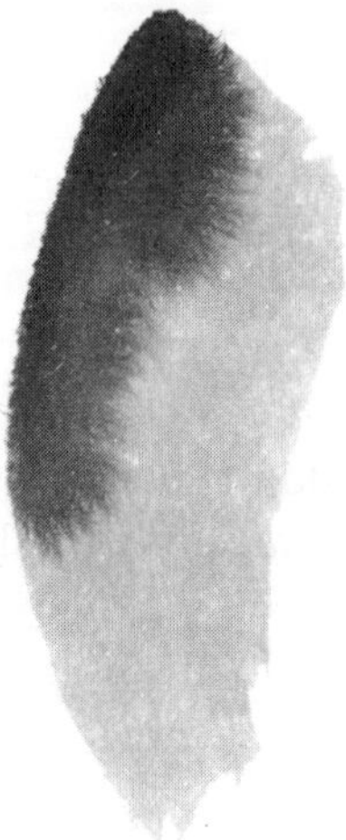

Nō-tan is also shown in the *kasure* or *nijimi* strokes.

Kasure

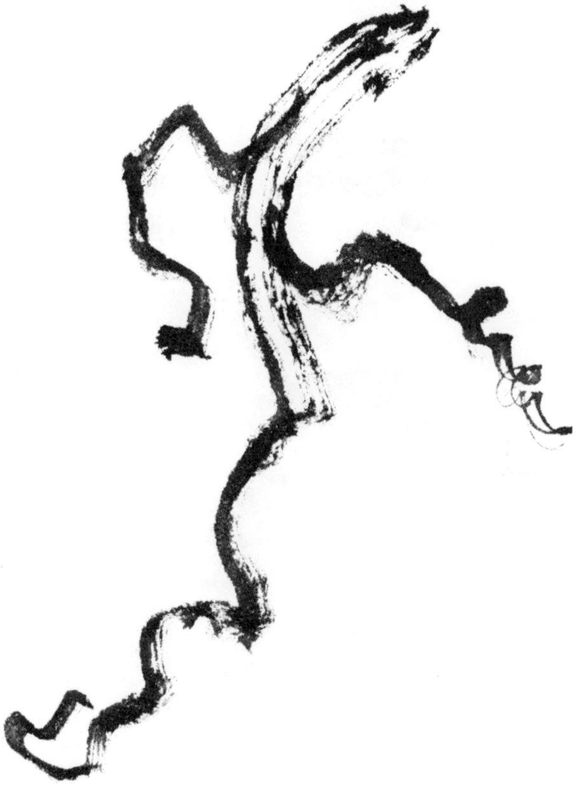

Kasure

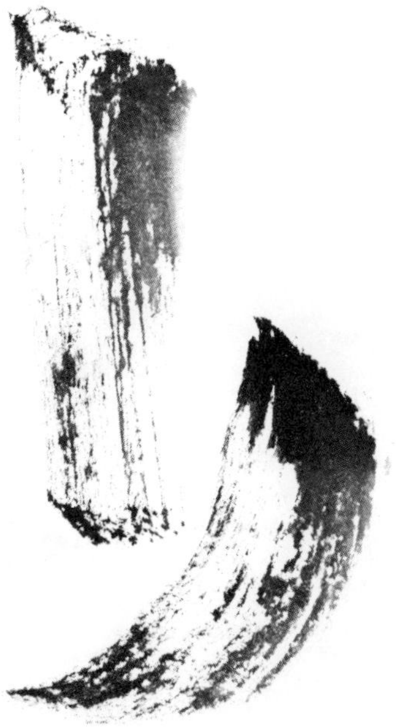

Nijimi

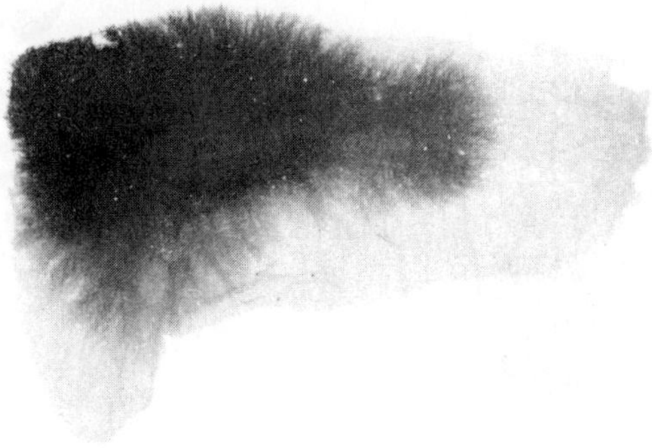

Remember the differences:

KASURE is made with a dry brush or with speedy movement and has a lacy effect.

NIJIMI is made with much moisture on your brush and has a blurred effect.

Lesson 5 - *Ten*

● Dots

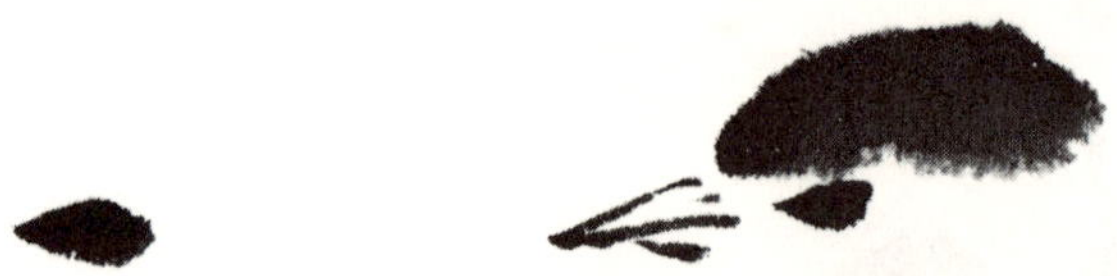

Bird's eye
(just press)

Beak

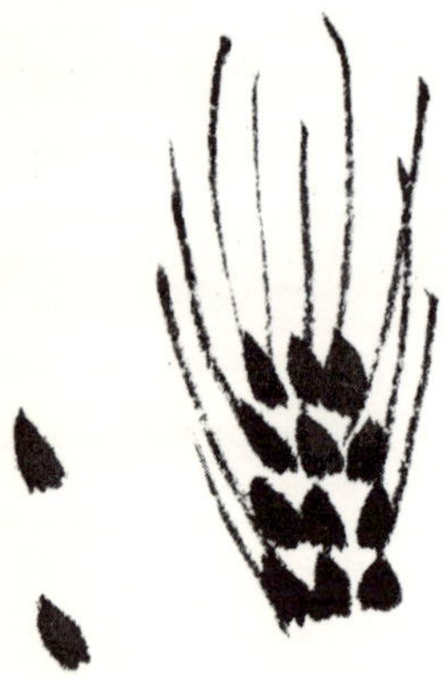

Grain

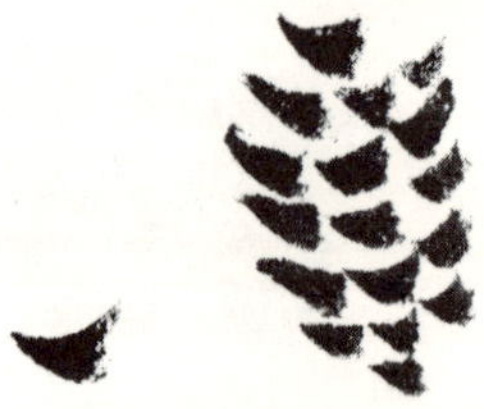

Pine cone

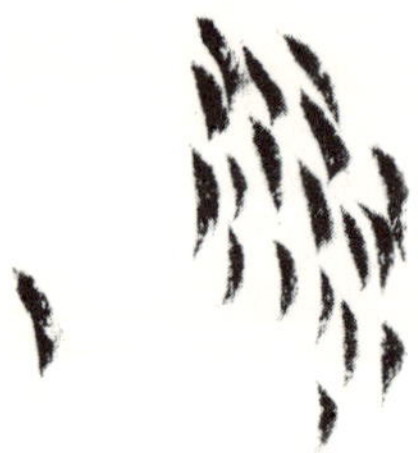

Narrow leaves

Examples for Practice

Bamboo (A)

Hold your brush straight up. Paint the branch first with light color ink, then each leaf from its base to its tip.

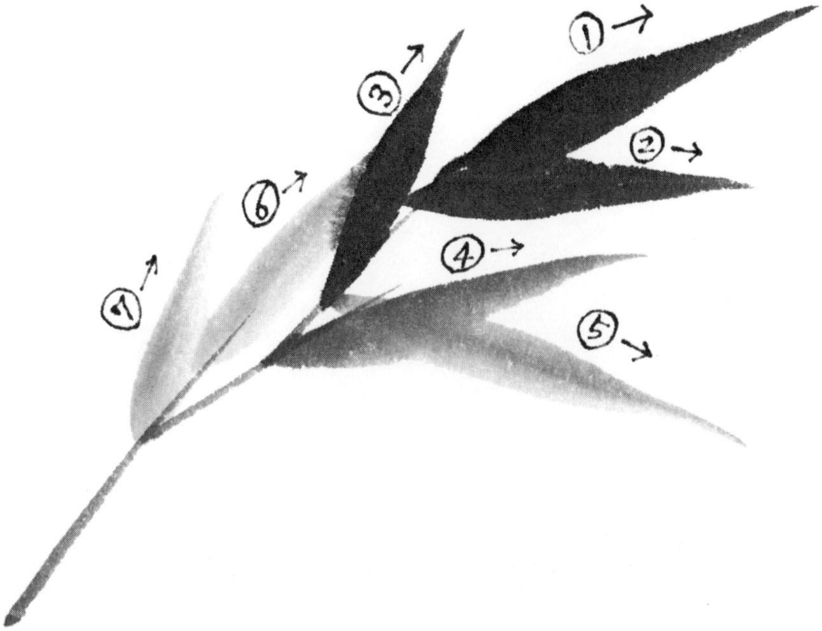

Branch

How to practice leaves

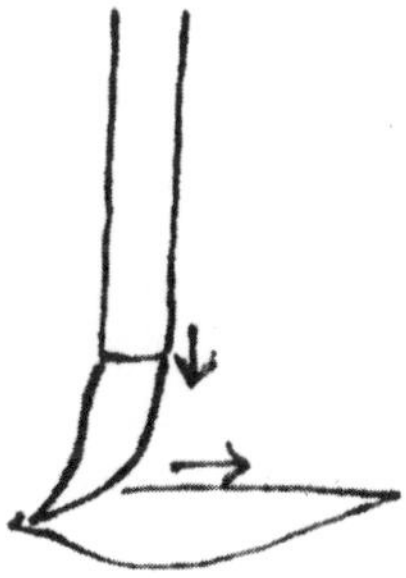

Press, pull, lift off

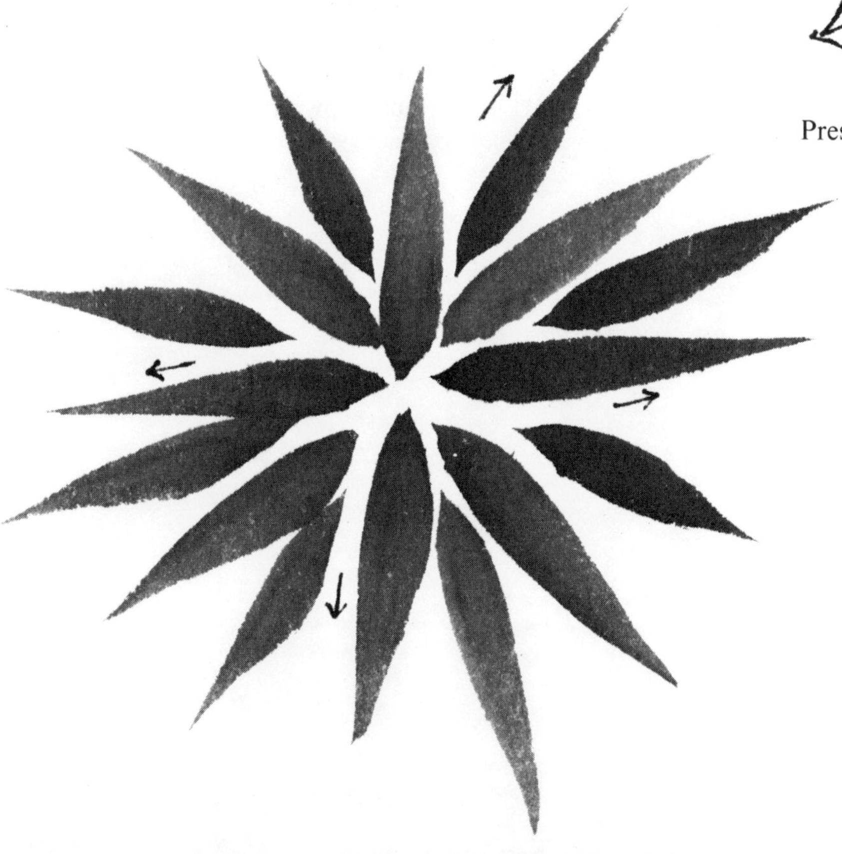

Bamboo (B) on a Fine Day

Trunk—First take up light color ink on your brush, then pick up dark color only at the tip.

(1) Press brush, pull downwards and lift off.
(2) Press, push upwards and press again.
(3) Press, push upwards and lift off.

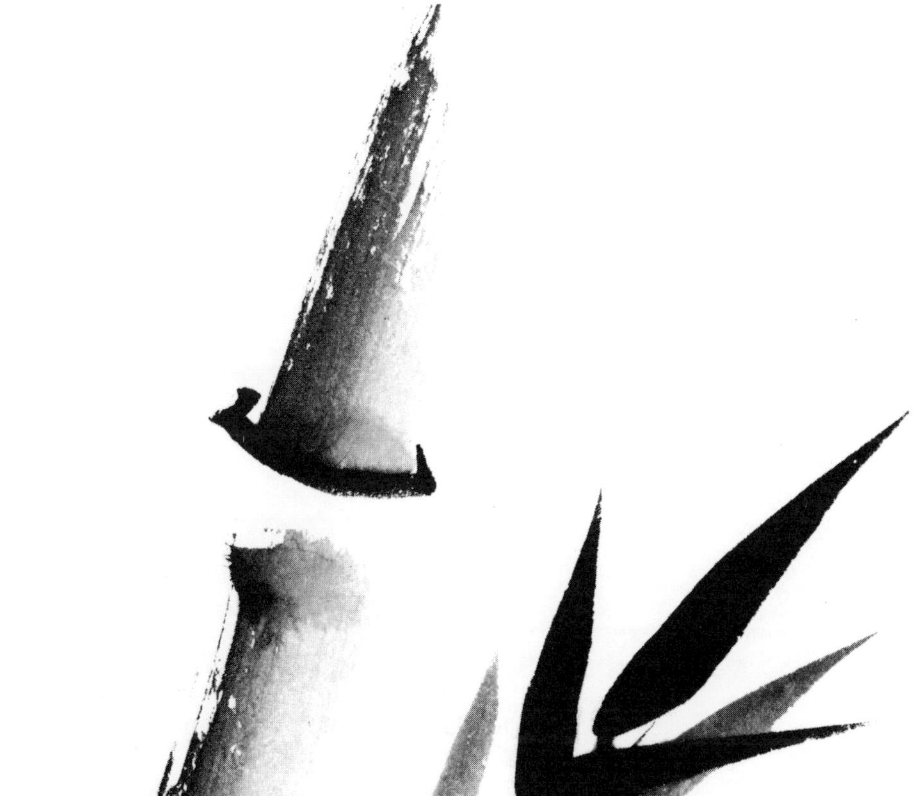
③
Trunk
②
①
Press
Lift off

Nodes—Use dark color ink. Holding your brush straight up, draw the nodes at the base of each section.

Branches—Use light color ink. Hold your brush straight up.

Small nodes—Use dark color ink.

Leaves—The order to draw is form the top leaf down to the bottom one. Each leaf is painted from the base at the branch to the tip. Use dark color ink which will gradually get lighter as you work down. If you must replenish your ink, use medium or light tone accordingly.

Branch with small node

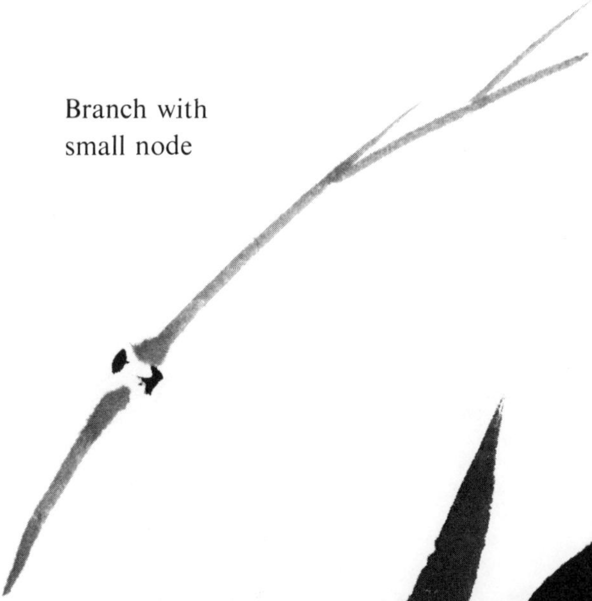

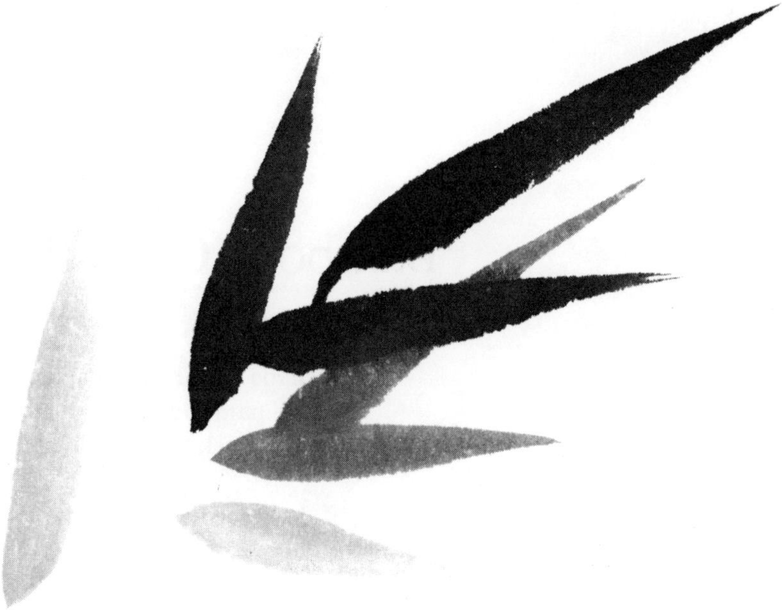

Leaves

Small node

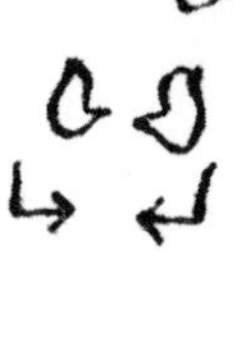

Large node

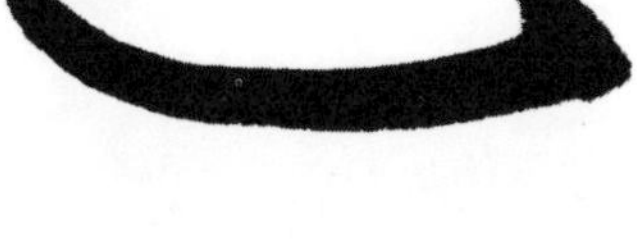

Bamboo (C) in the Rain

The shape of the leaves is enough to suggest rain without actually painting it. The order of drawing is the same, from the dark colored leaves to the light ones.

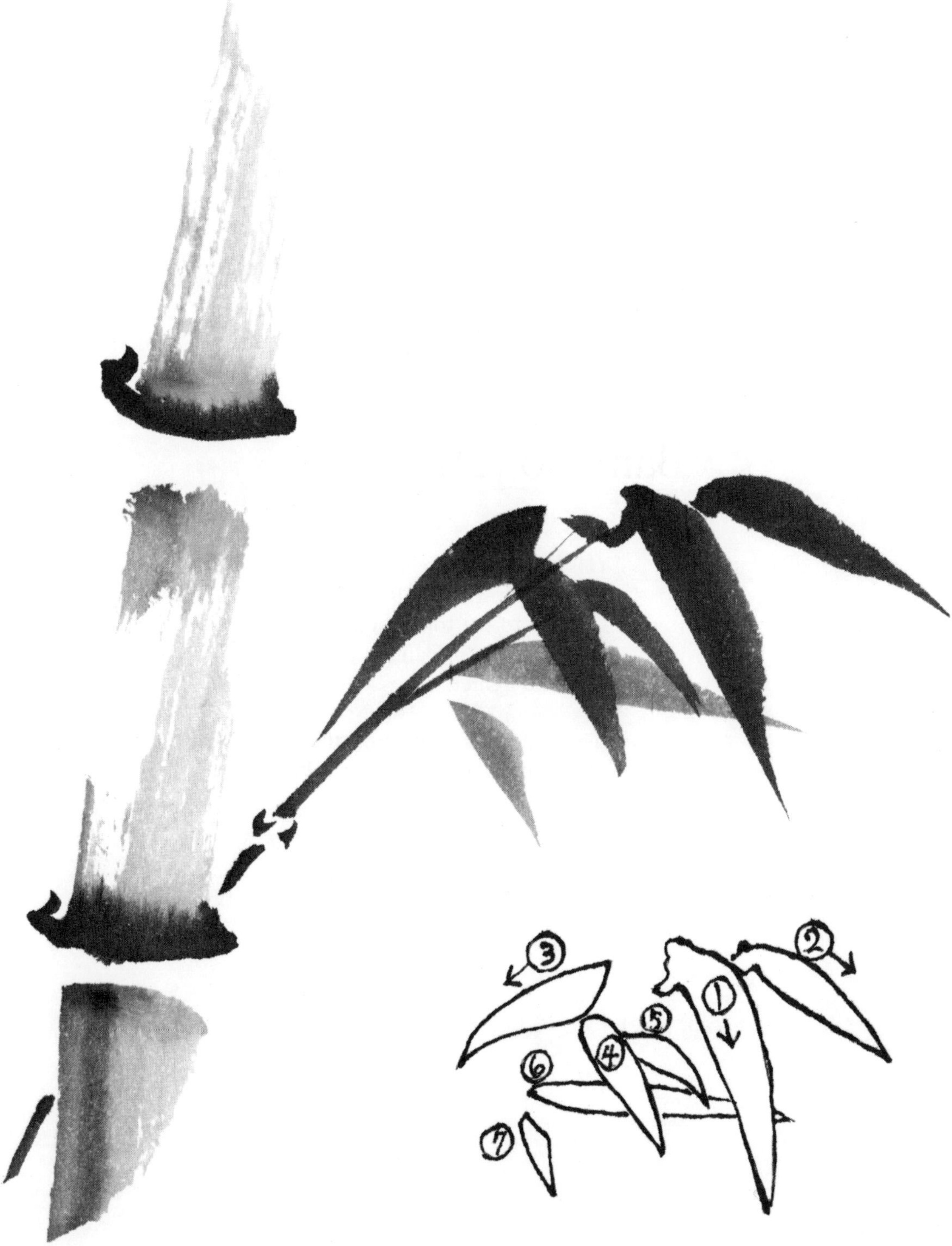

③
②
①
⑤
④
⑥
⑦

Bamboo (D)

(1) Again, branches are painted first, holding your brush straight up. Draw from the bottom, working up to the top, just as the bamboo grows.
(2) Leaves are painted from the dark colored ones to the lighter.

The bamboo is one of the trio of auspicious trees symbolizing happiness. The other two are the pine and the plum.

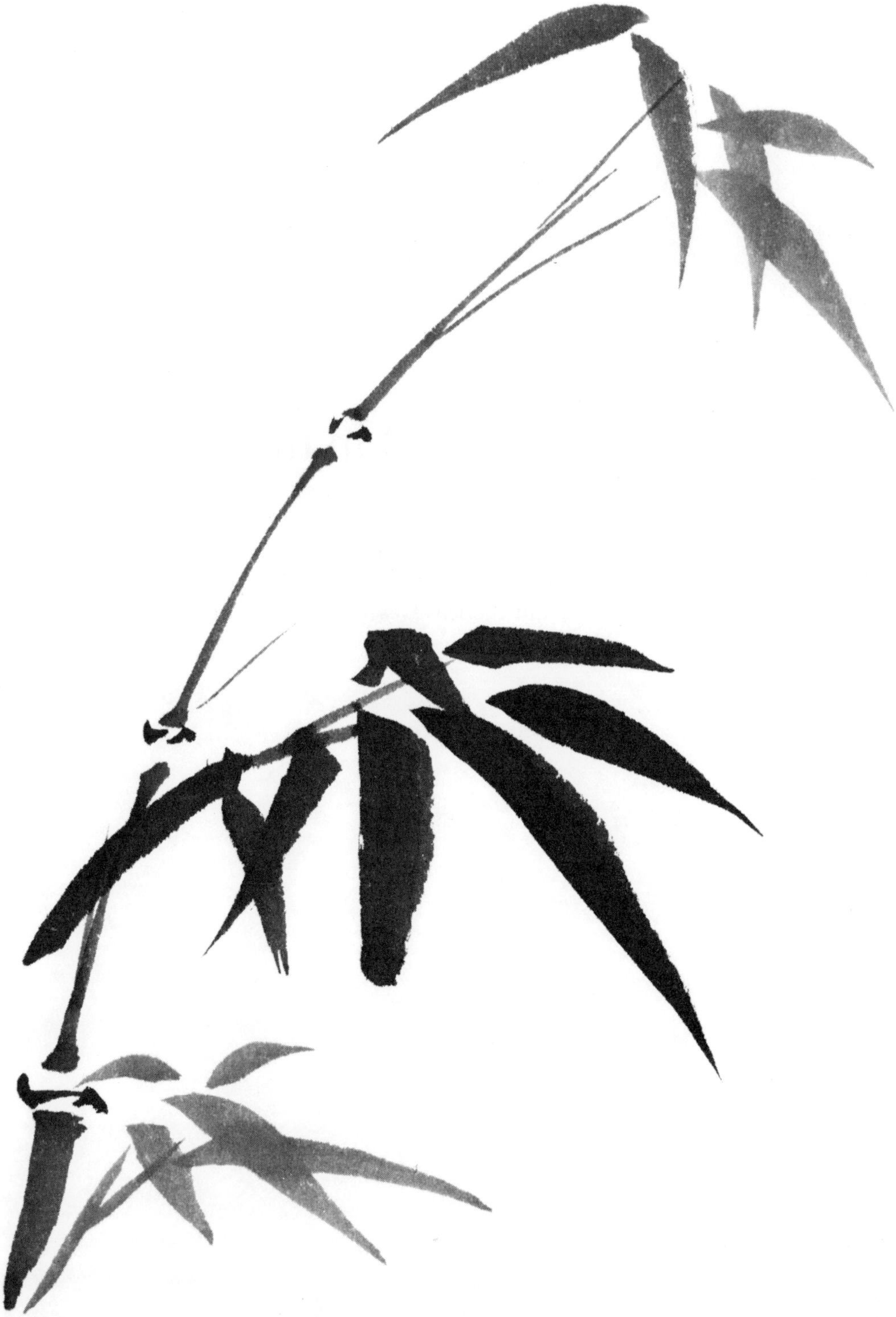

Bamboo (E) in the Wind

The contrast in color shows the difference in distance, the lighter colored leaves being blown farther away. Paint the leaves with the speed of the wind.

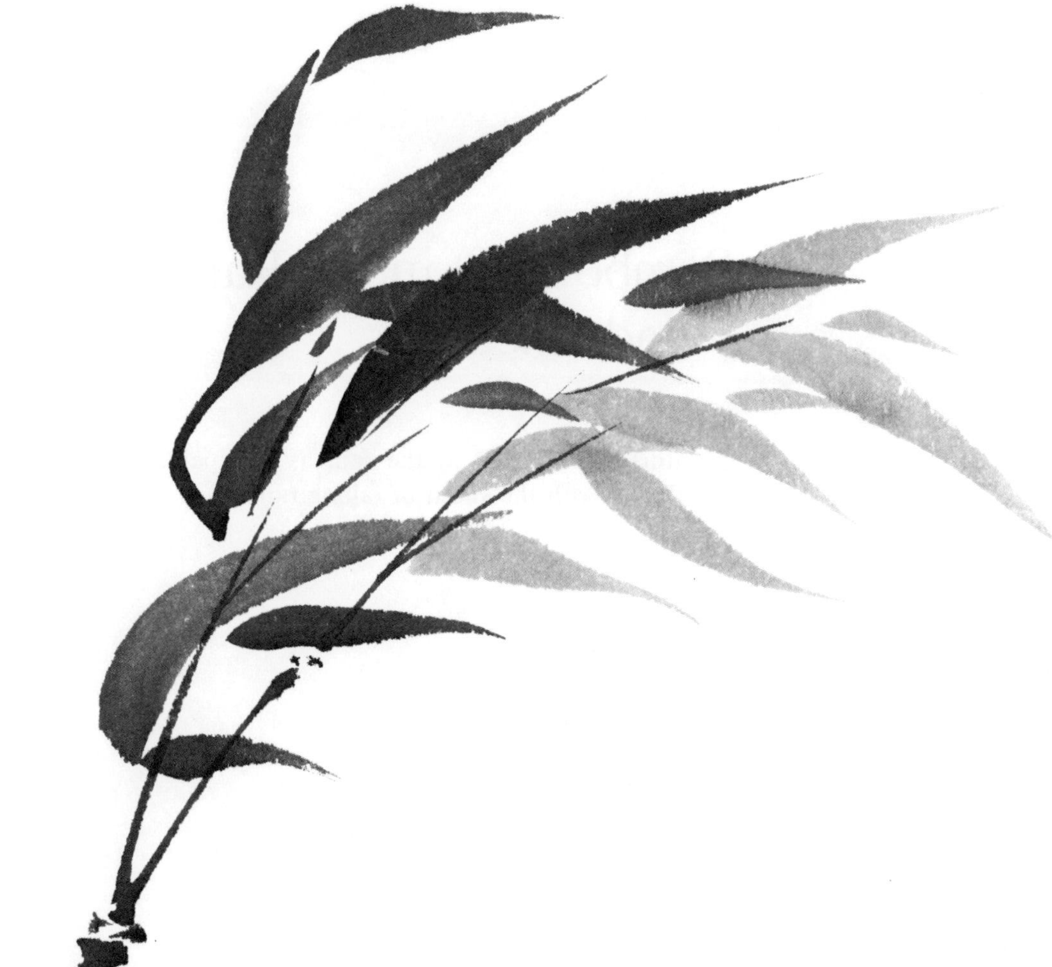

Bamboo (F) in the Rain (advanced)

Imagine yourself in the rain as you paint, drawing the leaves with the speed of falling rain.

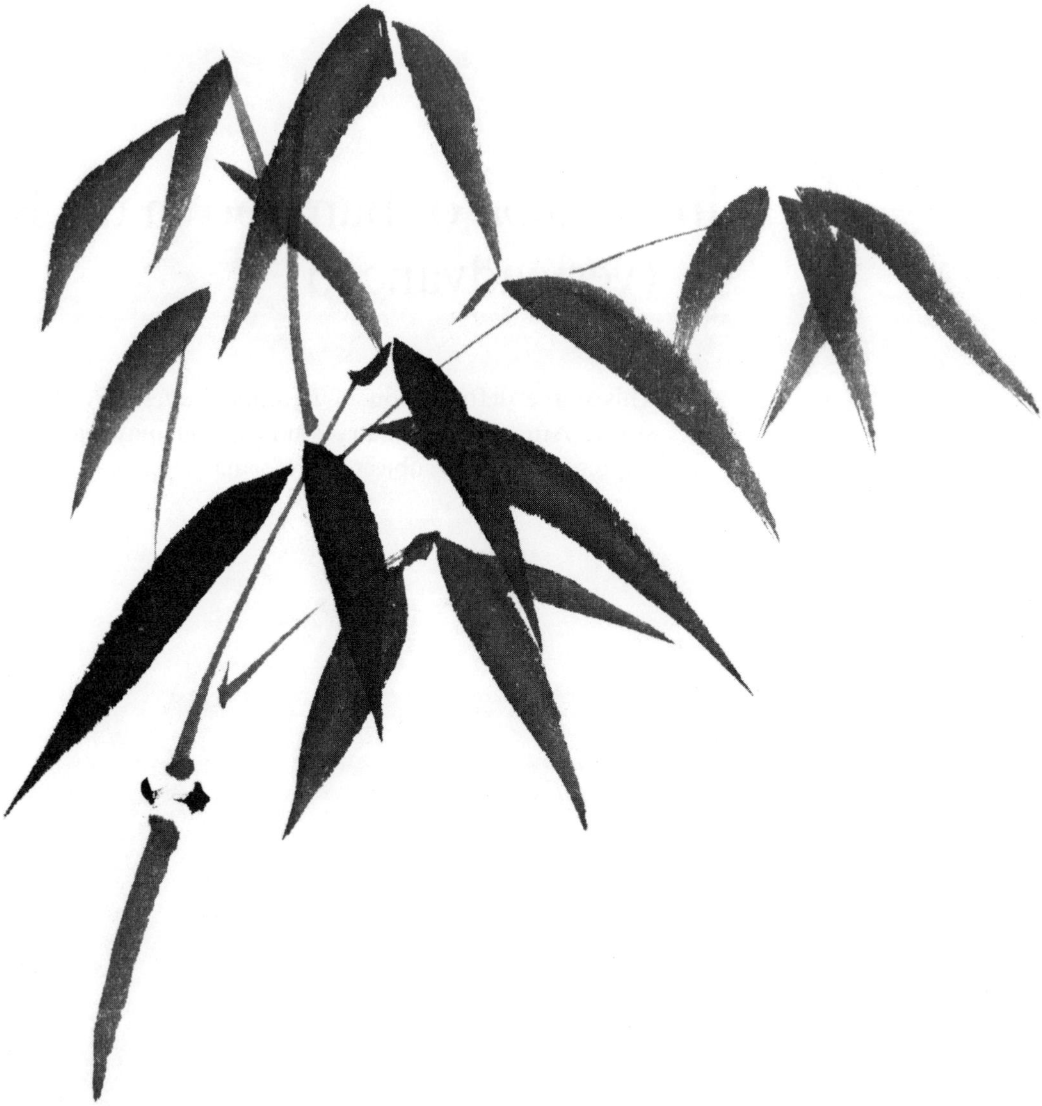

Impression of Bamboo in the Rain (very advanced)

This is the deformation of bamboo leaves for advanced study. After your primary studies, you may paint your impression of any subject in deformative style.

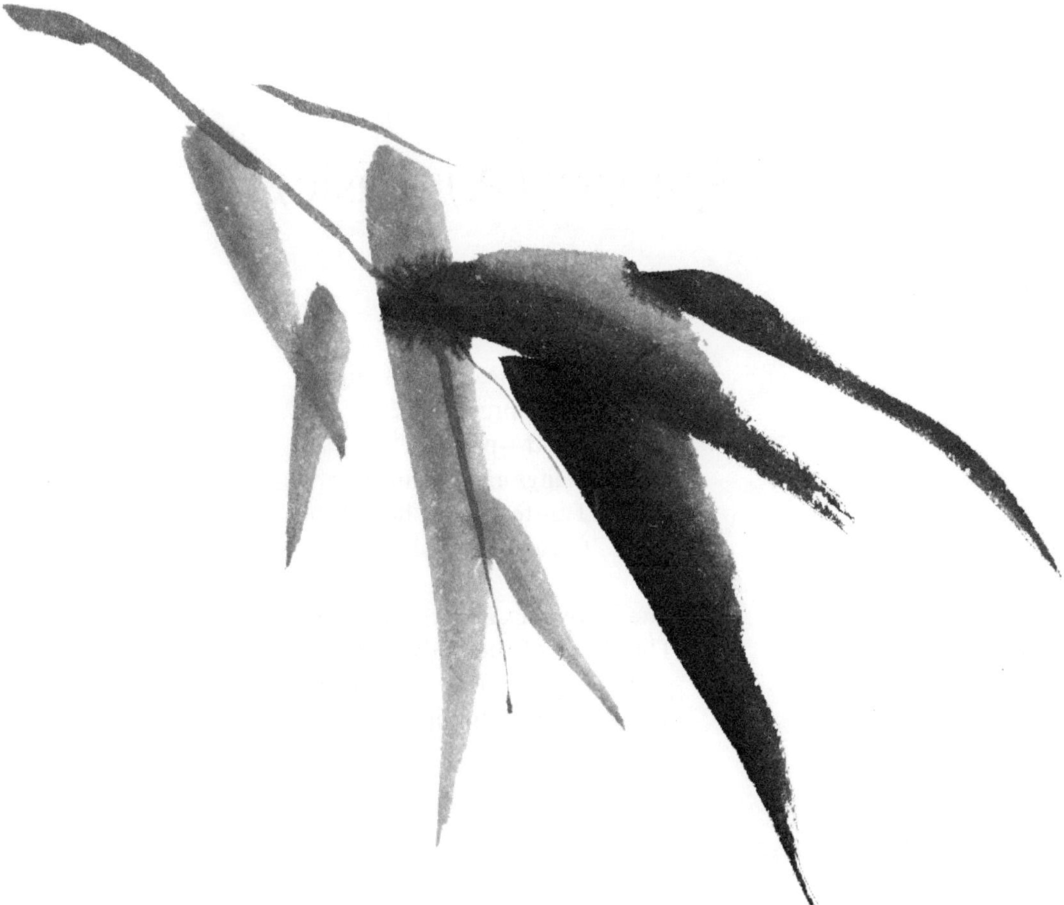

Sparrow (A) (basic)

Order to paint

(1) & (2) Beak—press lightly
(3) Eye—press lightly
(4) Head—press
(5) Wings and outline of body—hold brush straight up
(6) Tail feathers—hold brush straight up
(7) Claws—short line in center with dot on each side

The above examples are painted with simple outlines. The shape of the body is like that of an egg.

By giving him as much negative space as possible, you are permitting the little bird's freedom of movement—his existence.

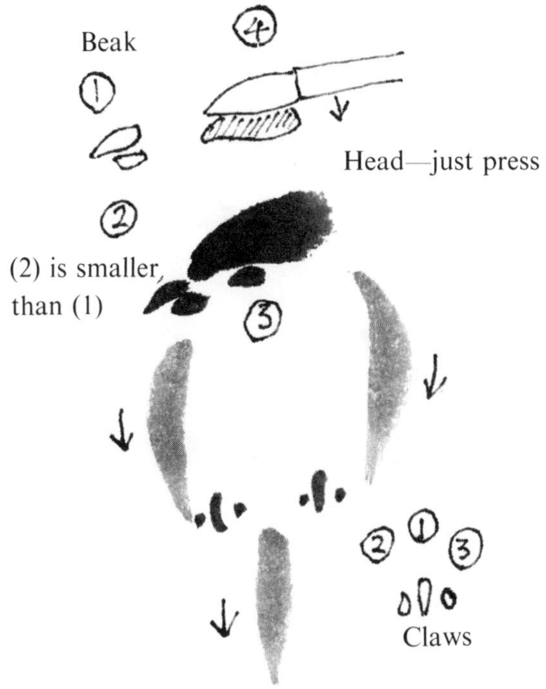
Beak
④
①
Head—just press
②
(2) is smaller than (1)
③
② ① ③
Claws

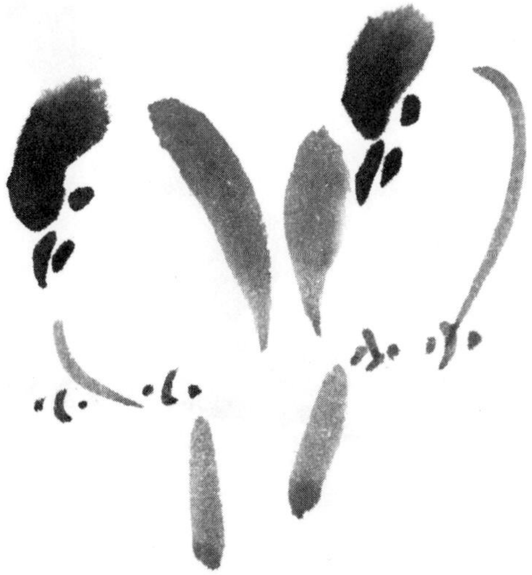

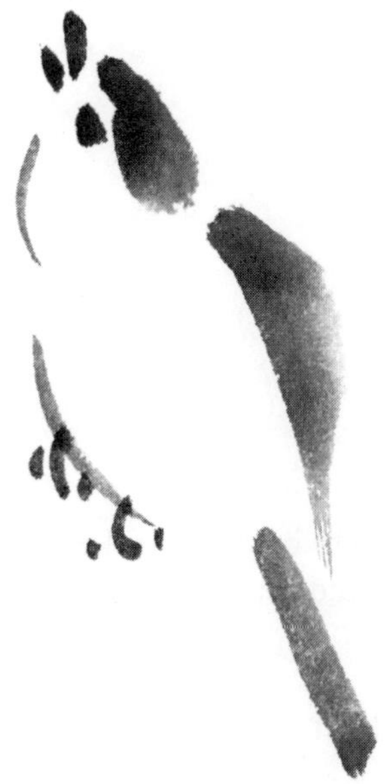

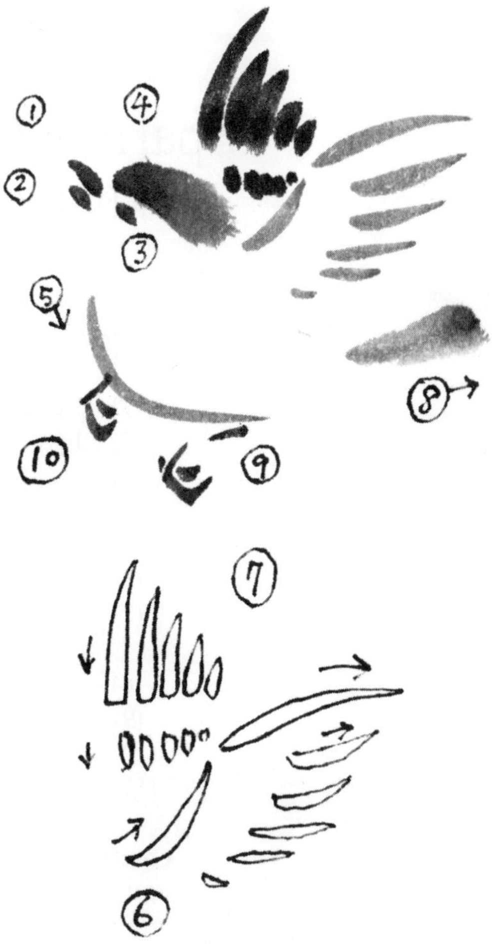
①
④
②
③
⑤
⑧
⑩
⑨
⑦
⑥

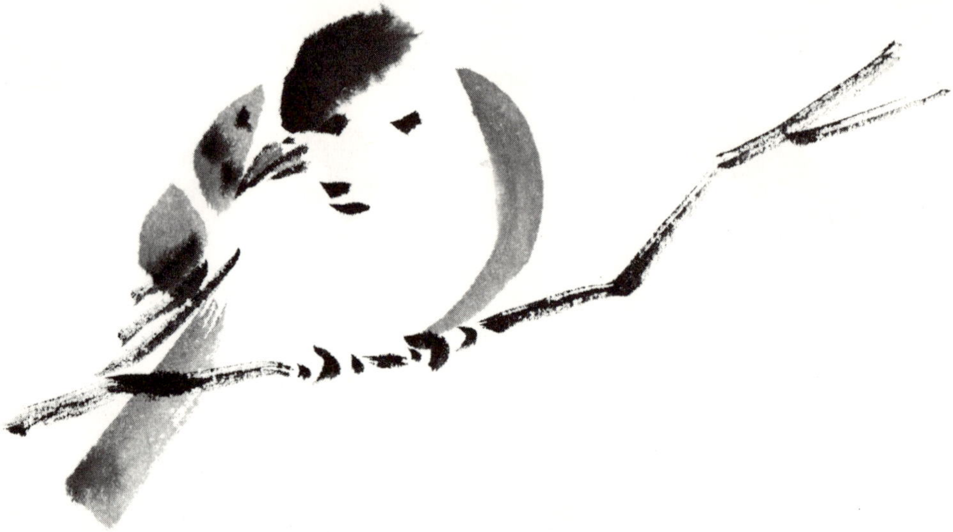

Sparrow (B) Sitting on a Branch (advanced)

Order to paint

(1) Beak outline
(2) Eye
(3) Head
(4) Dot behind eye
(5) Dots under beak
(6) Outline of body
(7) Back and wing—light colored strokes followed by dark colored dots and lines
(8) Tail feathers
(9) Claws
(10) Fill in beak with light color ink
(11) Branch

Carefully follow the different tones shown in these examples. The beak should be filled in last with light color.

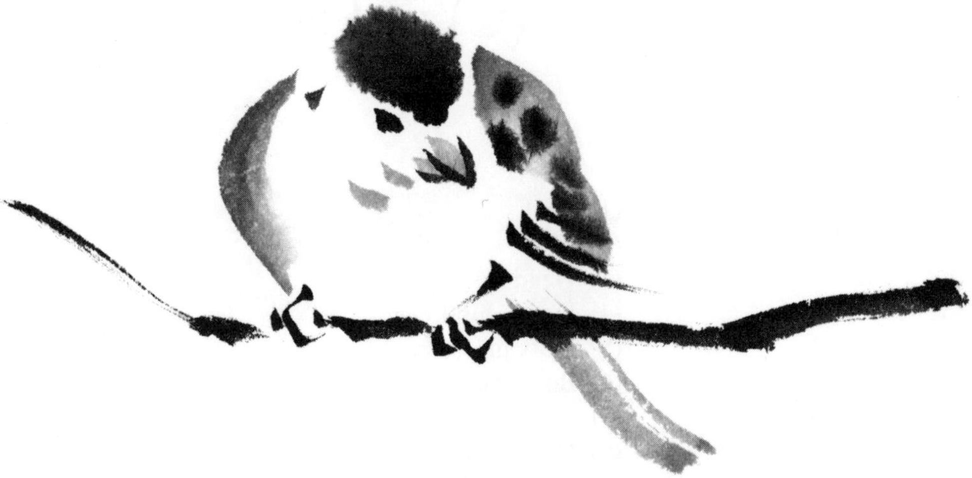

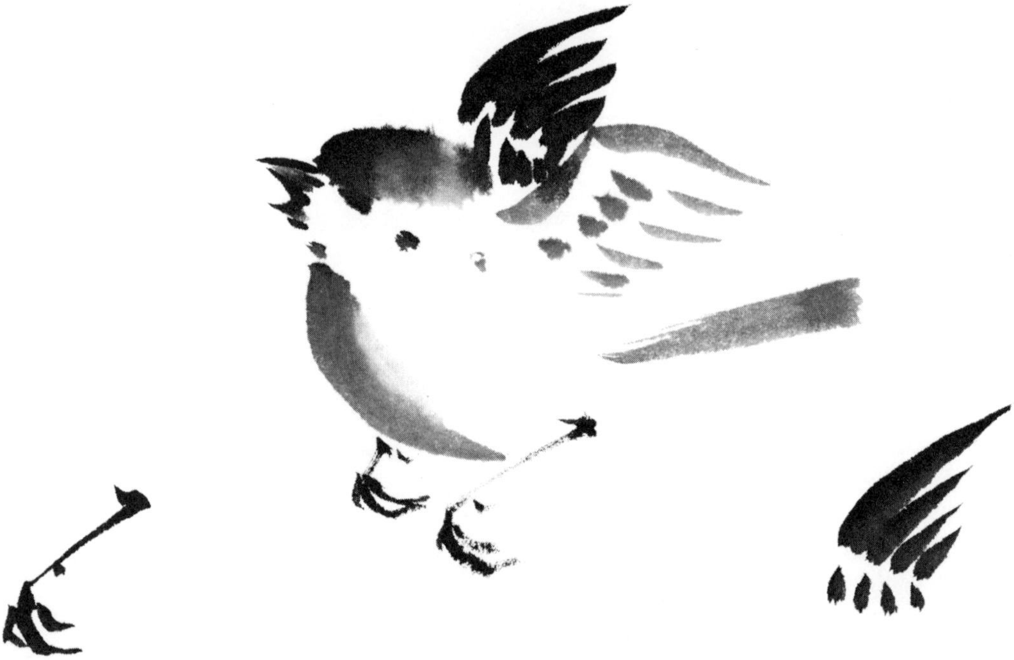

Sparrow (C) in Flight

Order to paint

(1) Beak
(2) Eye
(3) Head
(4) Dot behind eye
(5) Dots under beak
(6) Body outline
(7) Light colored wing
(8) Dark colored wing
(9) Tail feathers
(10) Claws

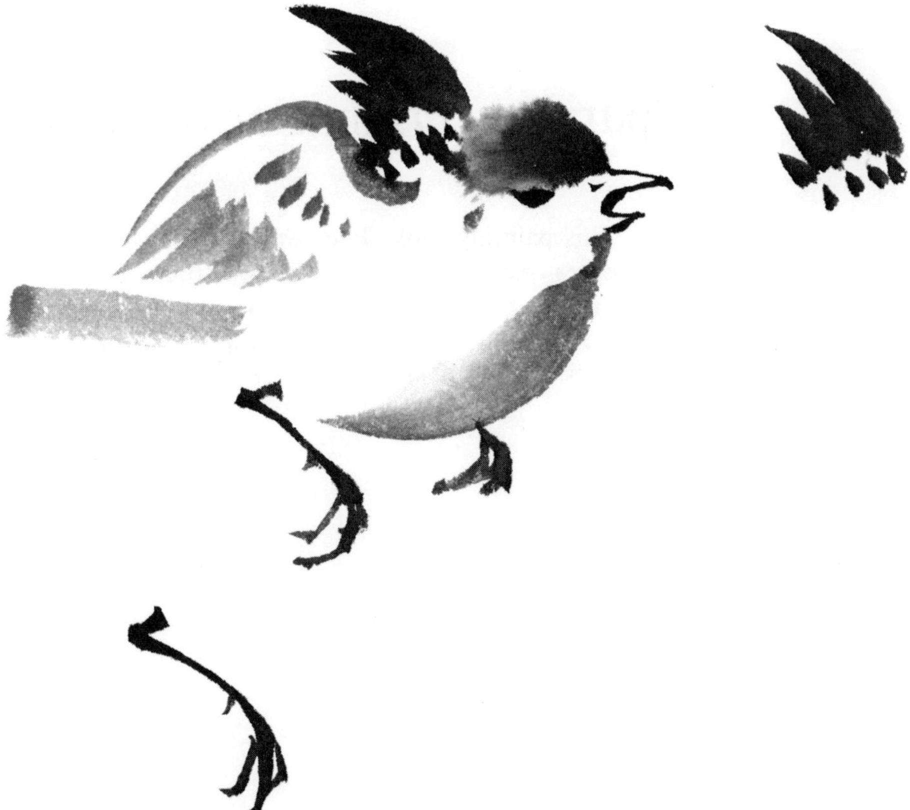

Sparrow (D) in Conversation

This painting looks like two birds conversing with each other. Actually, this example was prepared with the left-handed person in mind for whom the bird on the left would be easier to practice. However, it is also important to be able to paint any subject from any direction.

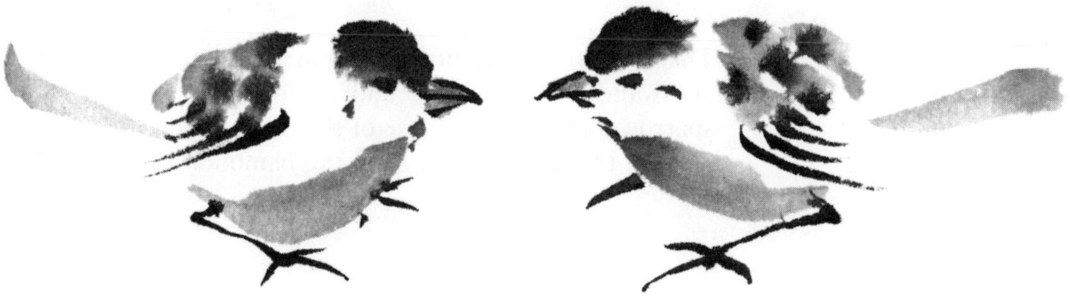

Combination of Sparrow (E) and Bamboo

There are many traditional combinations of subjects such as swallow and willow, and tortoise and crane. The sparrow and bamboo is one of the more popular of these.

Paint the sparrow first, then the bamboo.

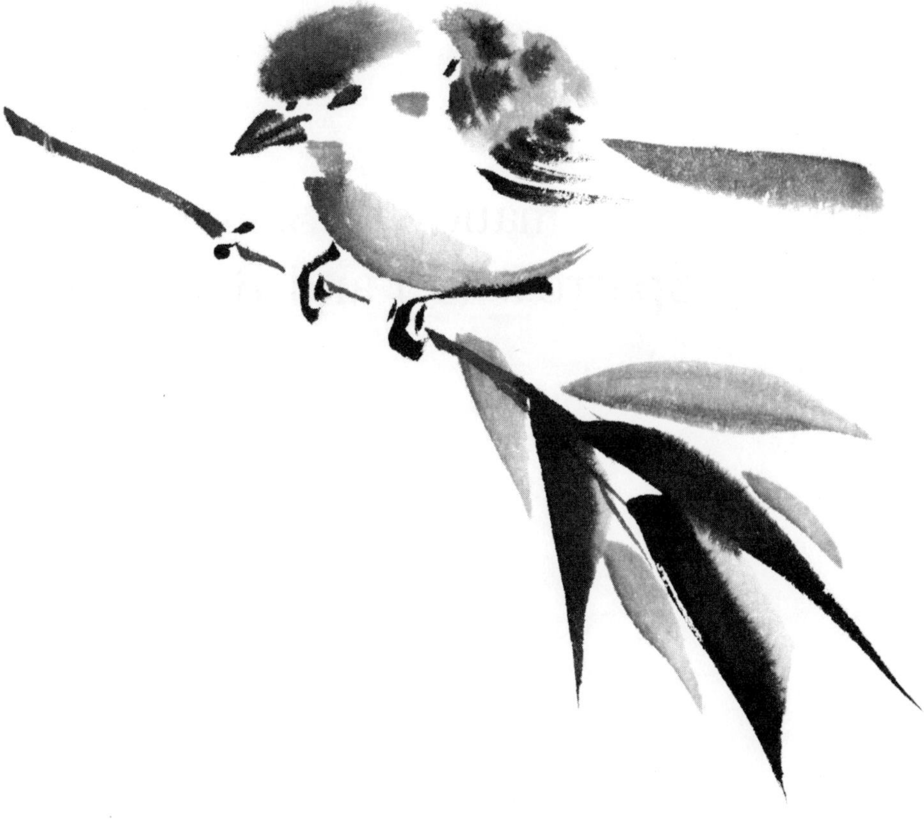

Sparrow (F) and Bamboo

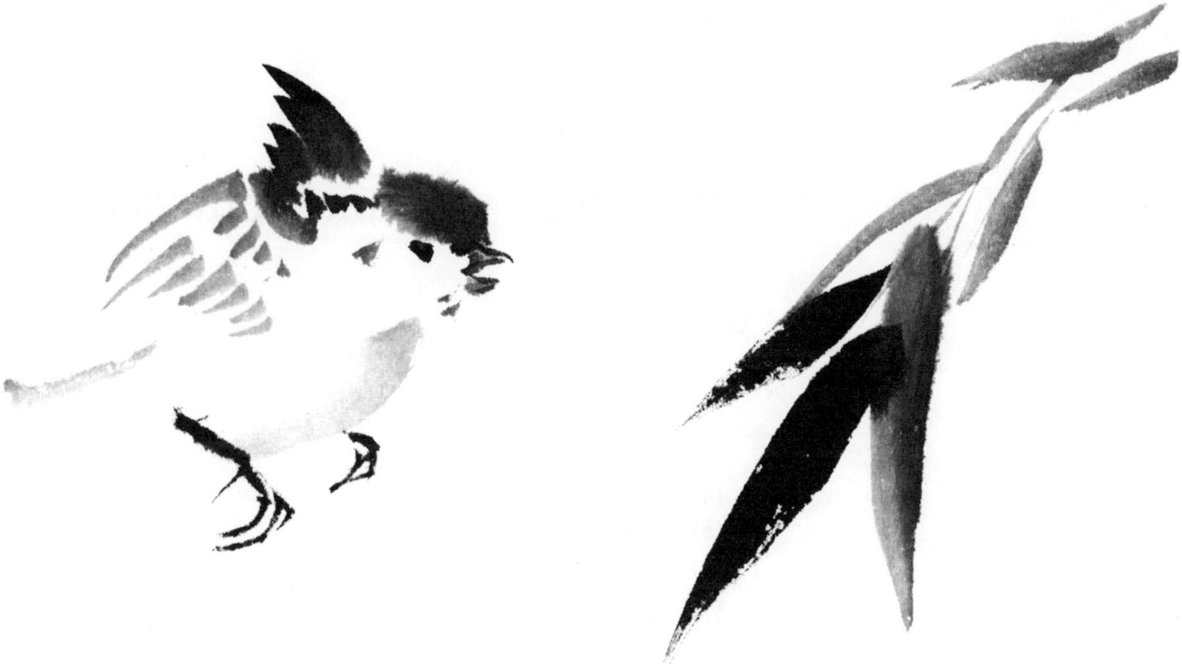

Sparrow (G) (detailed practice)

Order to paint

(1) Beak
(2) Eye and cheek
(3) Head
(4) Body
(5) Wings
(6) Tail feathers
(7) Claws

After painting the beak and eye with dark color, paint most parts with medium and light color ink. Then add some dark touches.

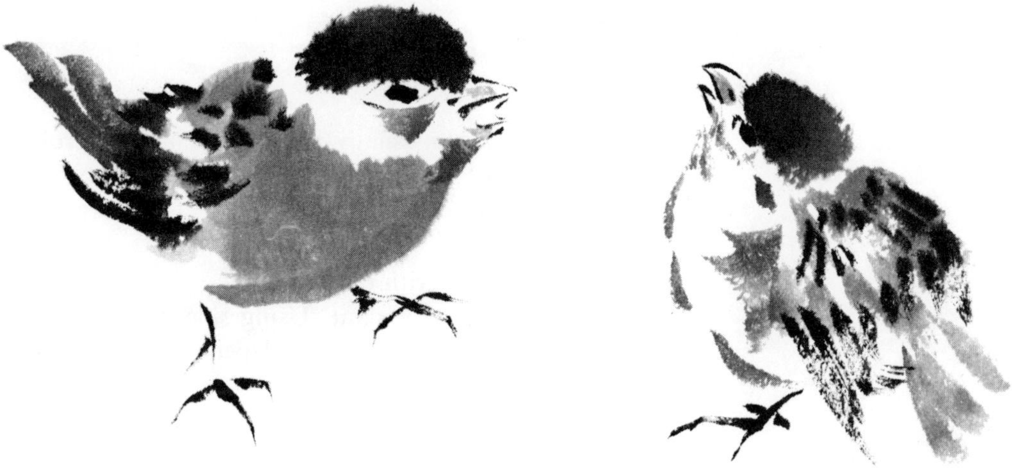

Leaves

This type of leaf can usually be painted in two strokes. By using different tones of ink and added accents, numerous variations are possible.

(1) Paint branch with dark ink.
(2) Hold brush at a slant. Using side of brush paint leaves in various tones depending on shading desired.
(3) Add veins in dark color.

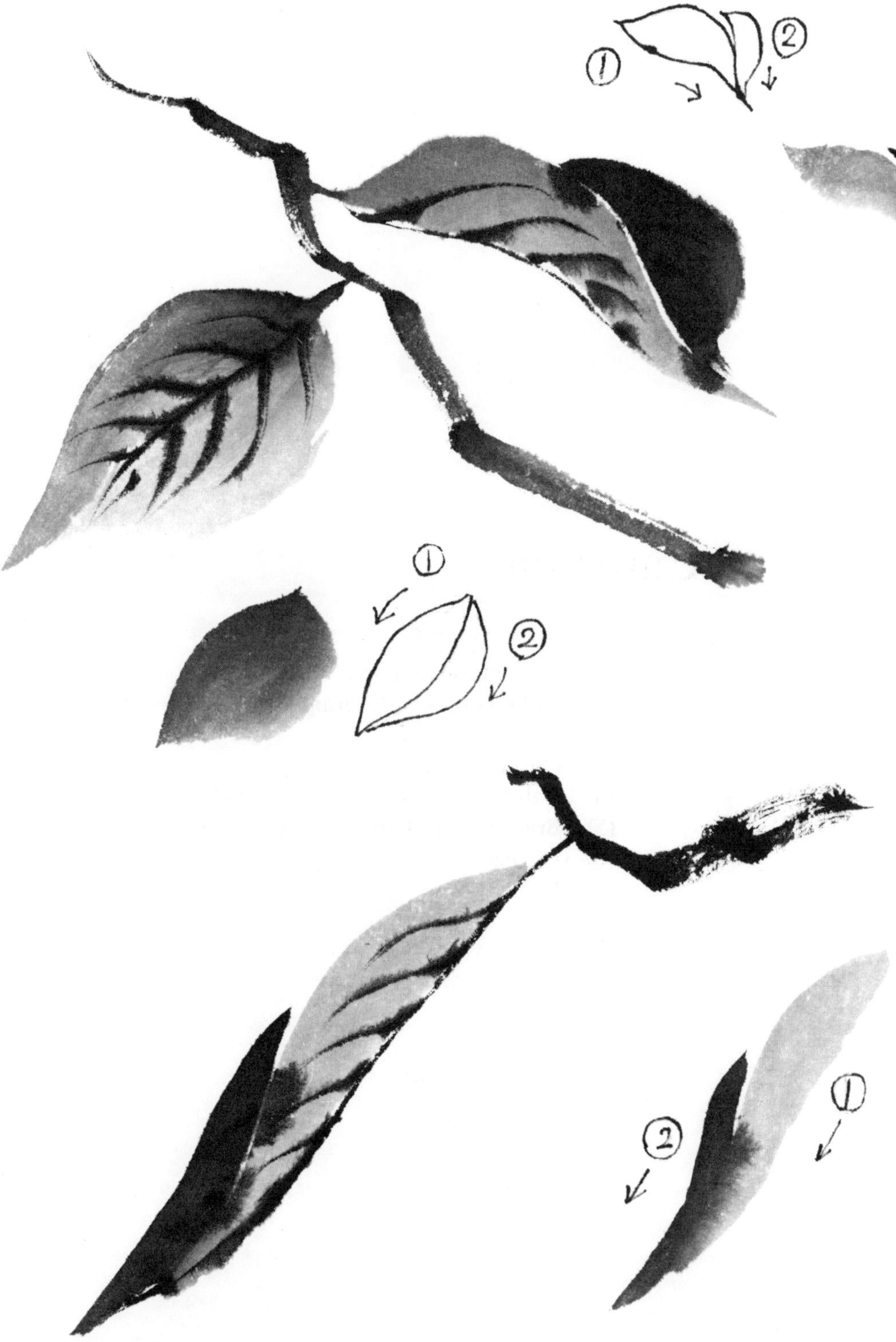
①
②
①
②
②
①

Camellia

(1) Stamens in dark ink.
(2) Hold your brush straight up and paint outlines of petals in light ink.
(3) Outline of bud.
(4) Calyx of bud using slanted brush.
(5) Branch in dark ink using dry brush.
(6) Leaves
(7) Veins

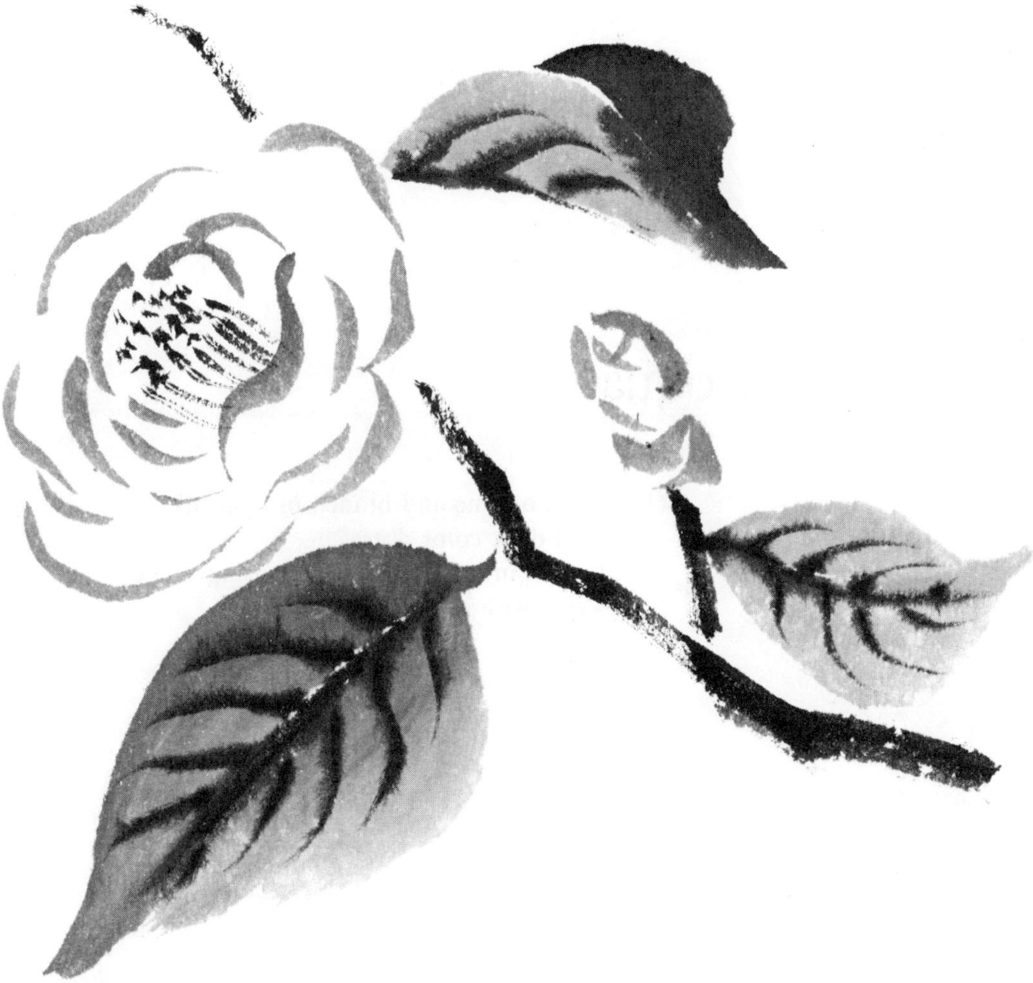

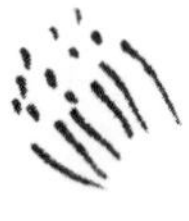

Stamens

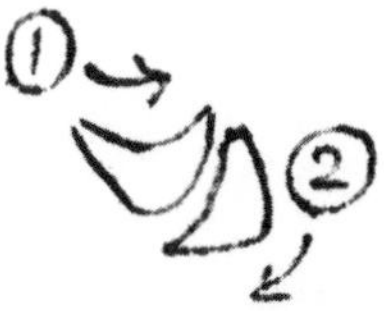

Calyx

Loquats

(1) Fruit outline and branch in light ink.
Add dark color dots.
(2) Leaves in two strokes each, using side of brush.
(3) Veins with dark ink.

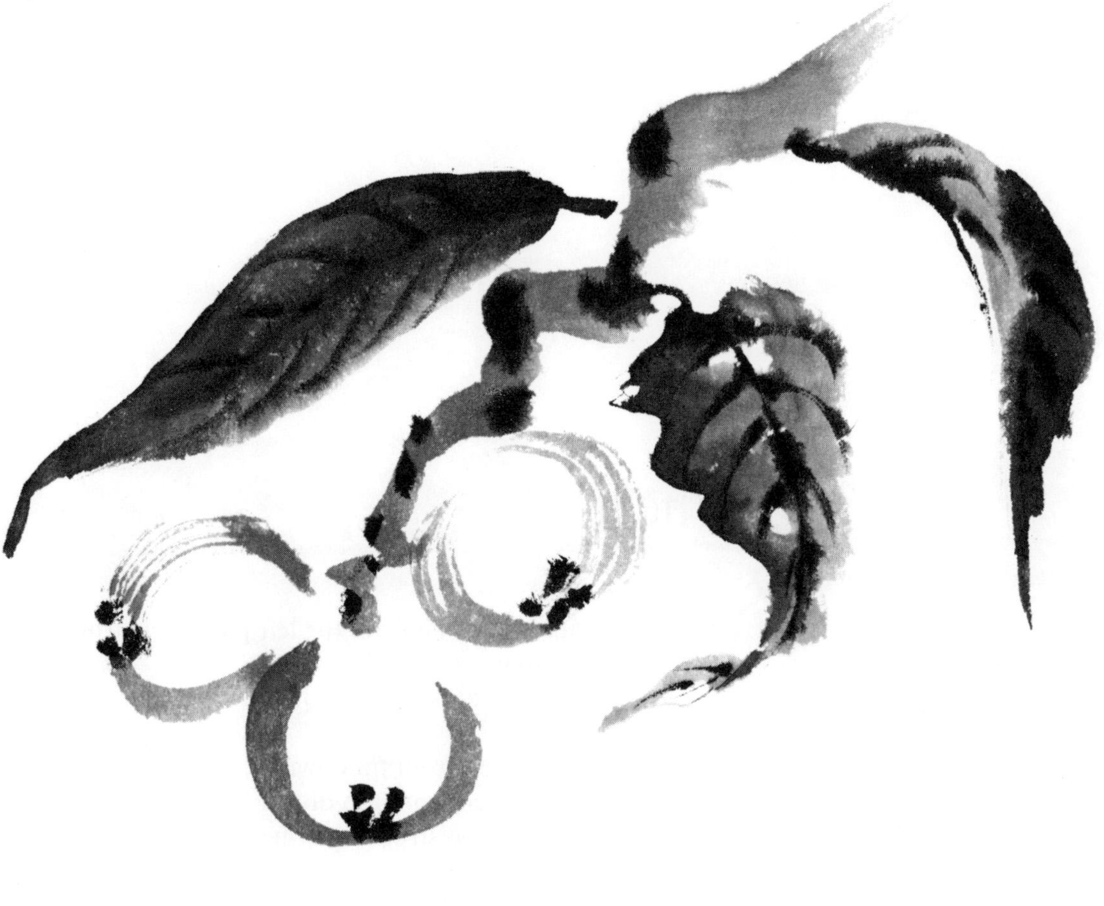

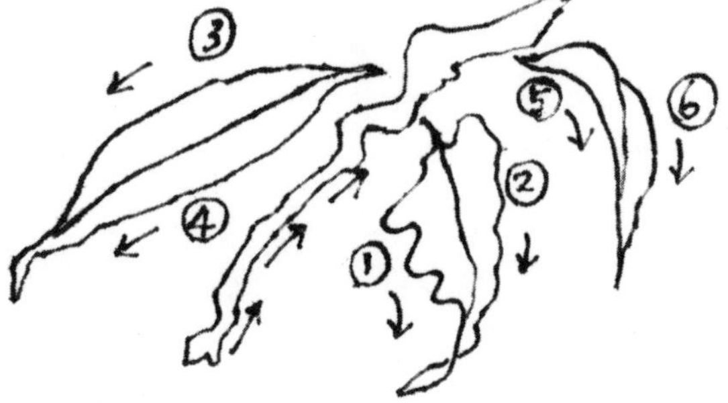

3
4
1
2
5
6

Wheat

(1) Grains—starting from the left paint dots from top to bottom.
Start with dark ink which will get lighter as you proceed.
(2) Ears painted from tip down.
(3) Stem painted from top down.
(4) Leaves in one stroke from bottom to top, holding brush straight up.
(5) Add veins last with dark ink.

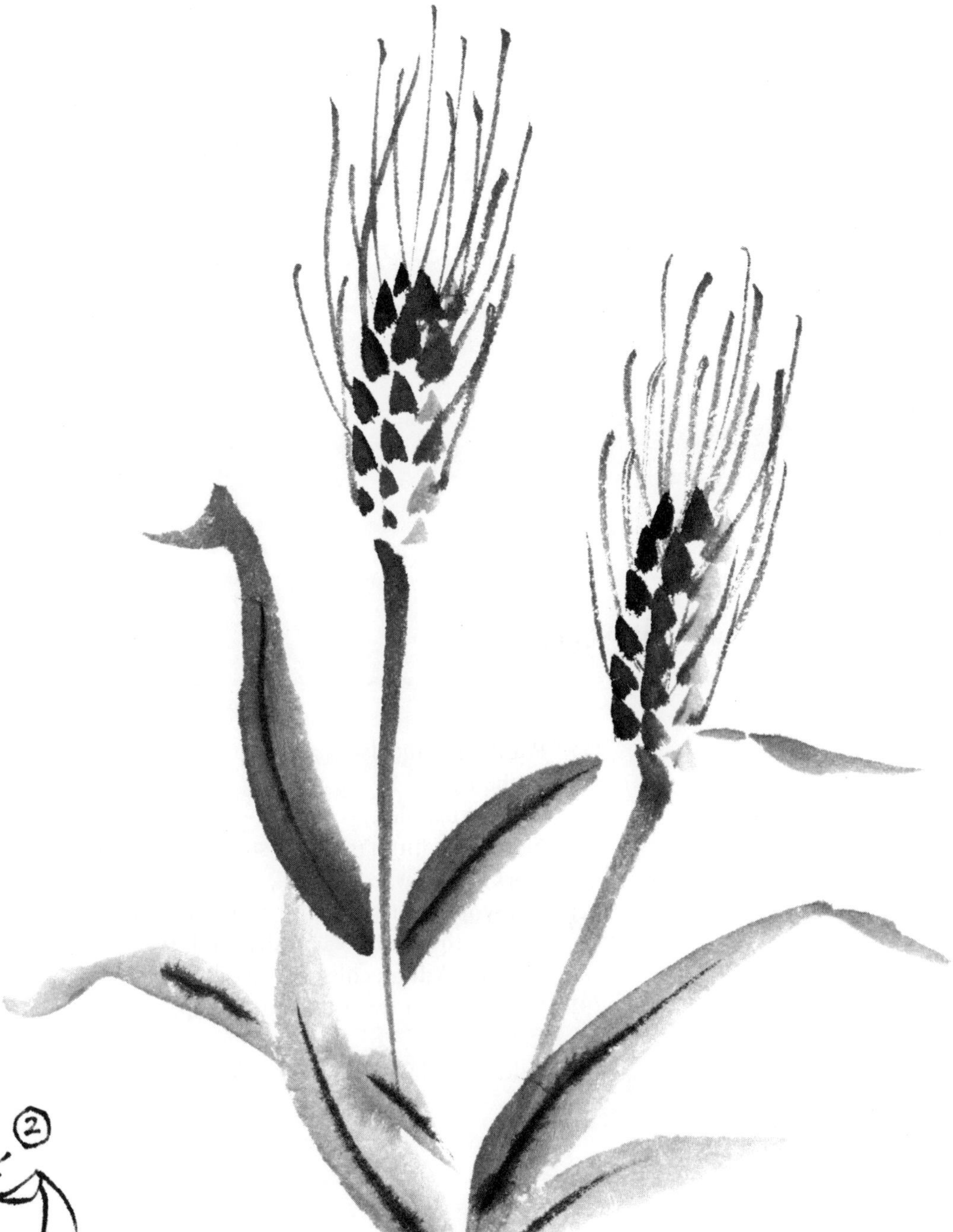

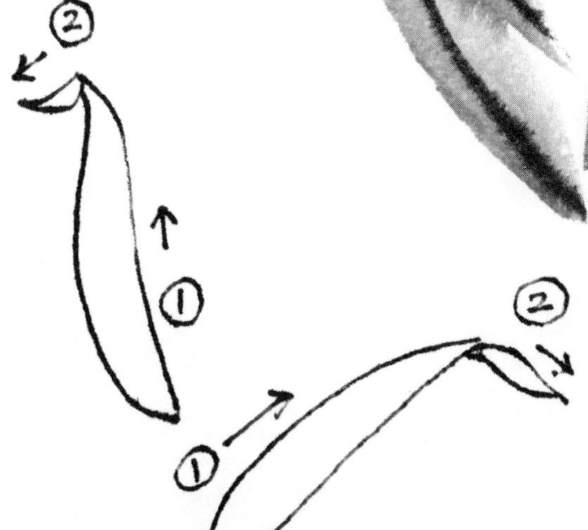
②
①
②
①

Chestnut

(1) Paint ripe nut using wet brush with dark ink only at the tip.
Hold brush flat.
Needles with dark ink starting from the inside working outwards.

(2) For young chestnut use wet brush with dark ink at the tip, hold vertically and twist in circular motion. Add needles in dark ink.

(3) Paint branch from bottom to top.

(4) Leaves

(5) Add veins last with dark ink.

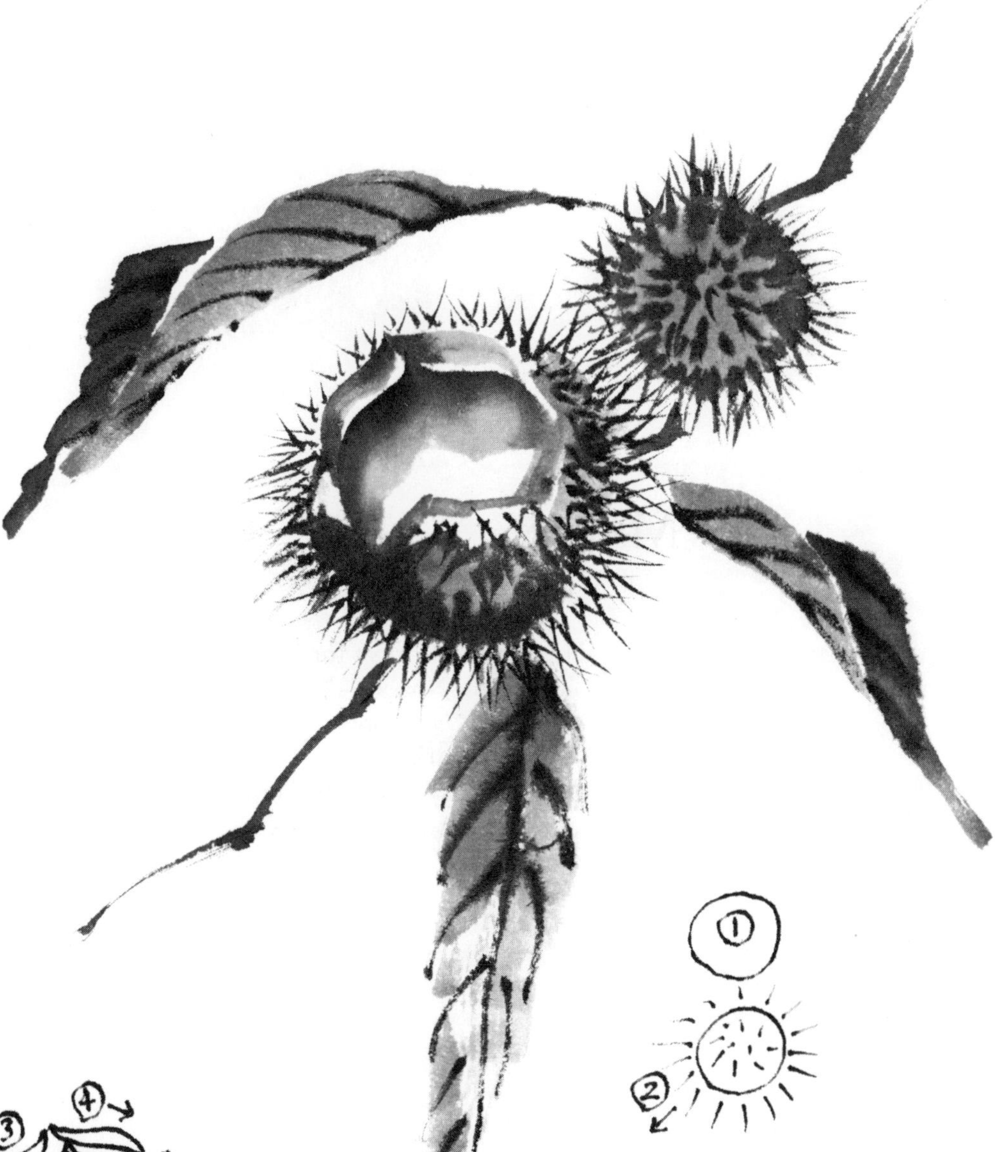
1
2

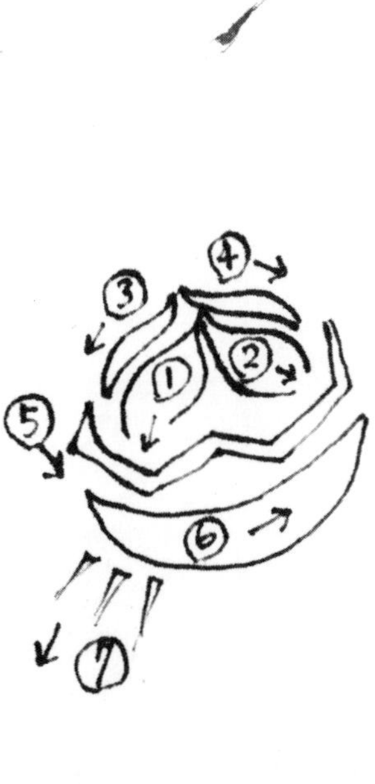
4
3
1
2
5
6
7

Maple

(1) Use wet brush for leaves.
Paint Nos. ①–⑤ from inside to outside, Nos. ⑥ and ⑦ just press from outside to inside. Add veins with dark ink.

(2) Use dry brush for branch painting from top to bottom with dark ink.

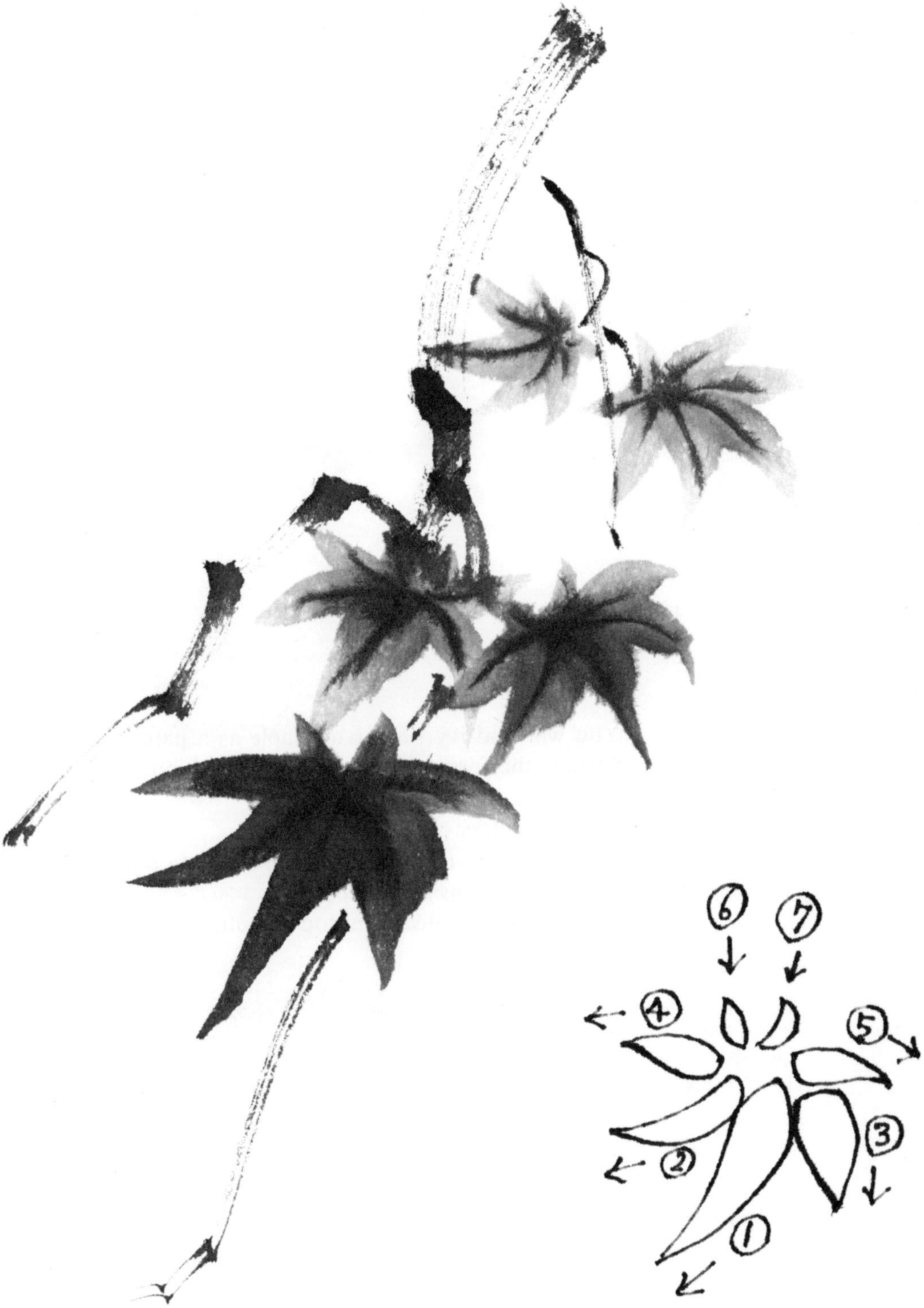
6
7
4
5
3
2
1

Ivy

You will find ivy similar to maple as a painting subject. Change the forms of the vines for variation.

(1) Paint leaves with wet brush.
Slant brush, painting from inside to outside.
Add veins in dark color.
(2) Vines painted from top to bottom.

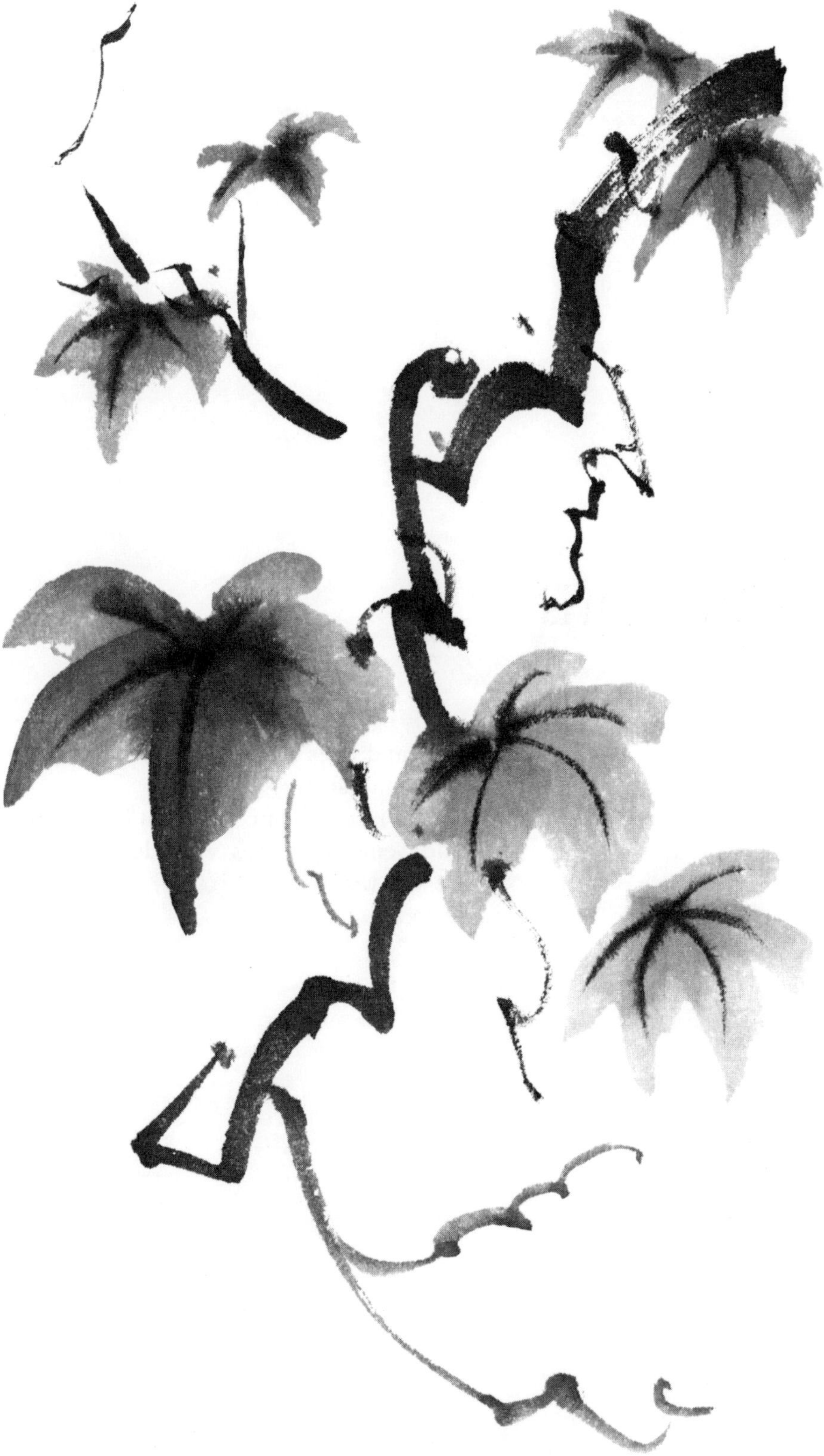

Iris

(1) Petals in medium color ink.
(2) Dots and lines on petals in dark ink.
(3) Calyx and stem.
(4) Leaves in medium color from bottom to top.
(5) Add veins on leaves with dark ink while leaves are still wet.

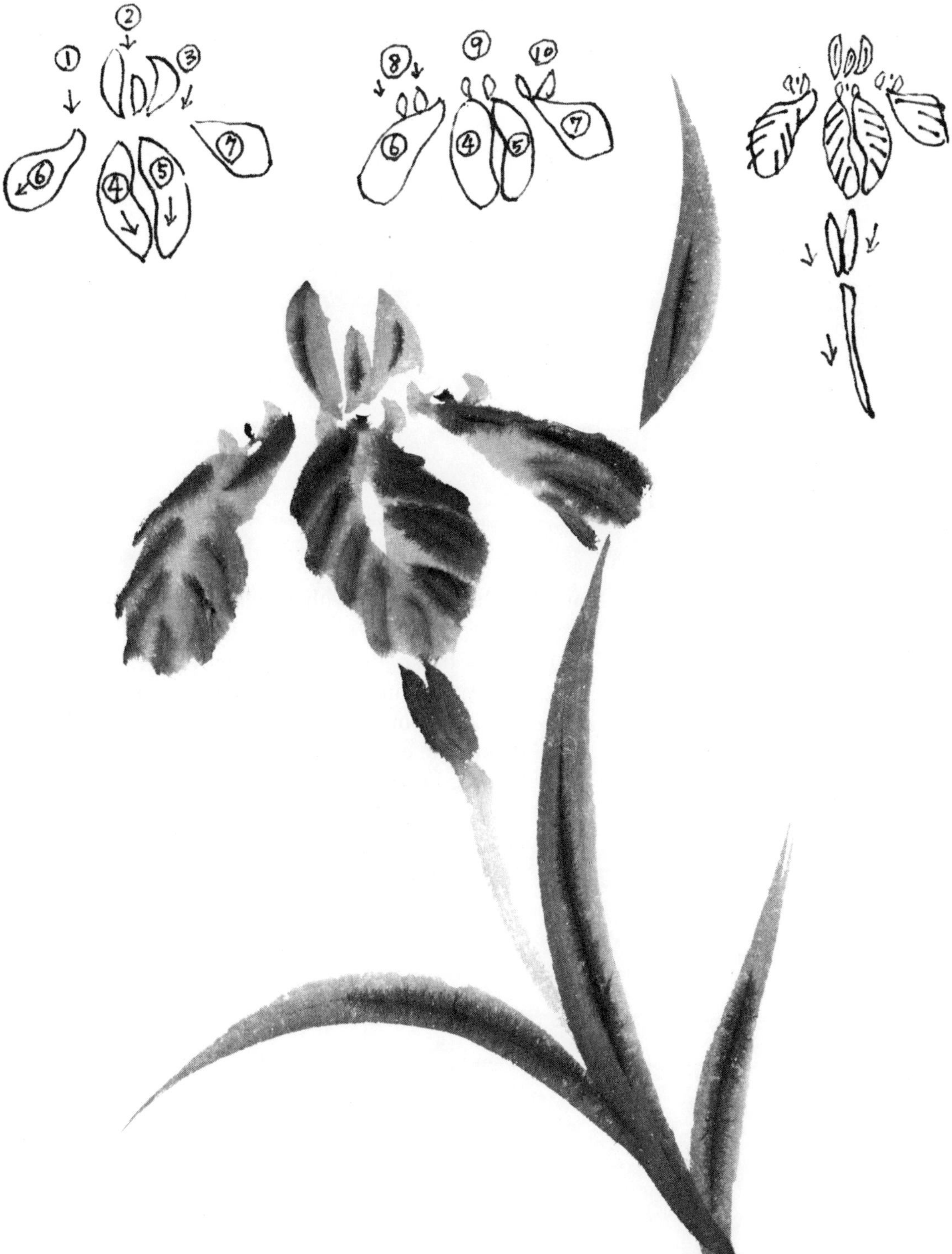

Fish

Paint the shaded stroke with a slight curve for fish.

(1) Wash brush thoroughly, removing excess water. Apply dark ink only to the tip. Use slanted brush, starting from the head.
(2) Paint the eye, mouth and gill using dark ink, holding brush straight up.
(3) Fill in around the eye with dark color.
(4) Add fins in medium ink.
(5) Add dark color lines to back and tail fins.

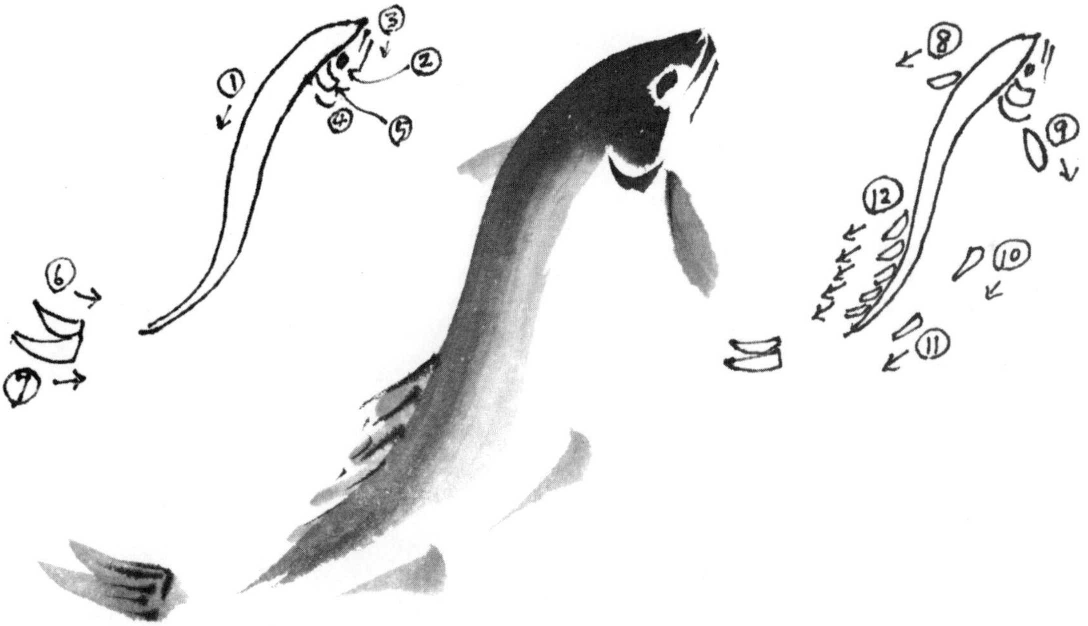
1
2
3
4
5
6
7
8
9
10
11
12

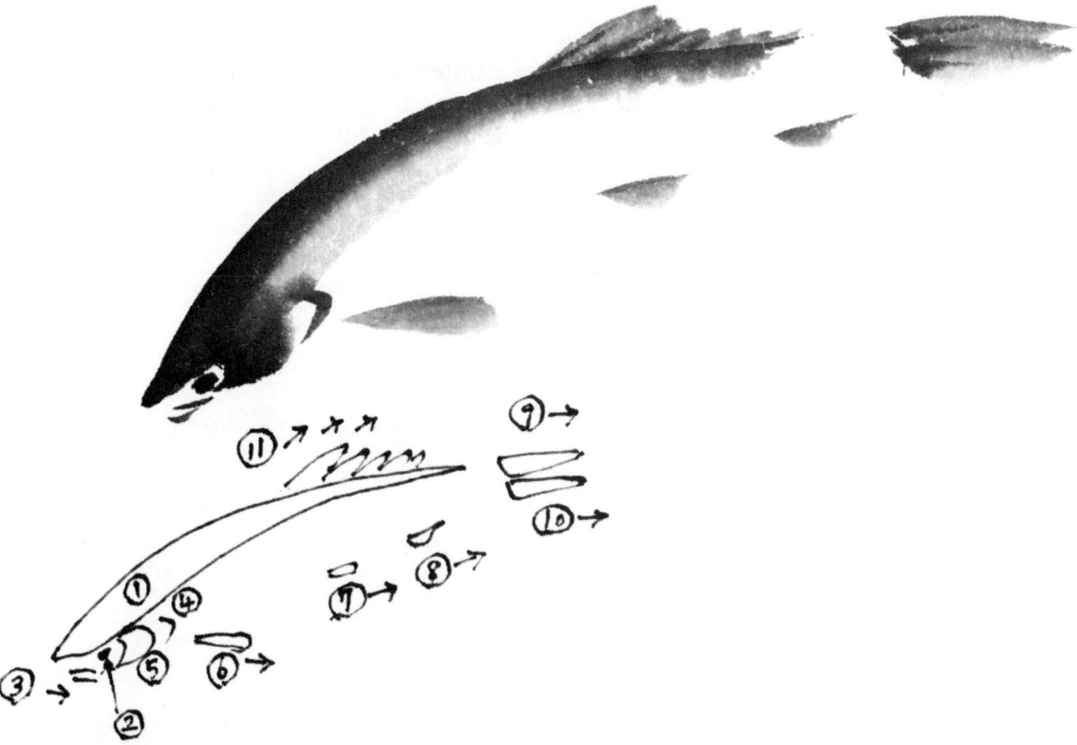
1
2
3
4
5
6
7
8
9
10
11

Crab

(1) Paint eyes with dark ink.
(2) Wash brush. Apply medium color ink thoroughly to brush, then add dark ink to the tip. Press several times between eyes, then paint shell holding brush slanted.
(3) Pincers painted in medium color.
(4) Paint each leg in one stroke from the body outwards, pressing slightly at each section.

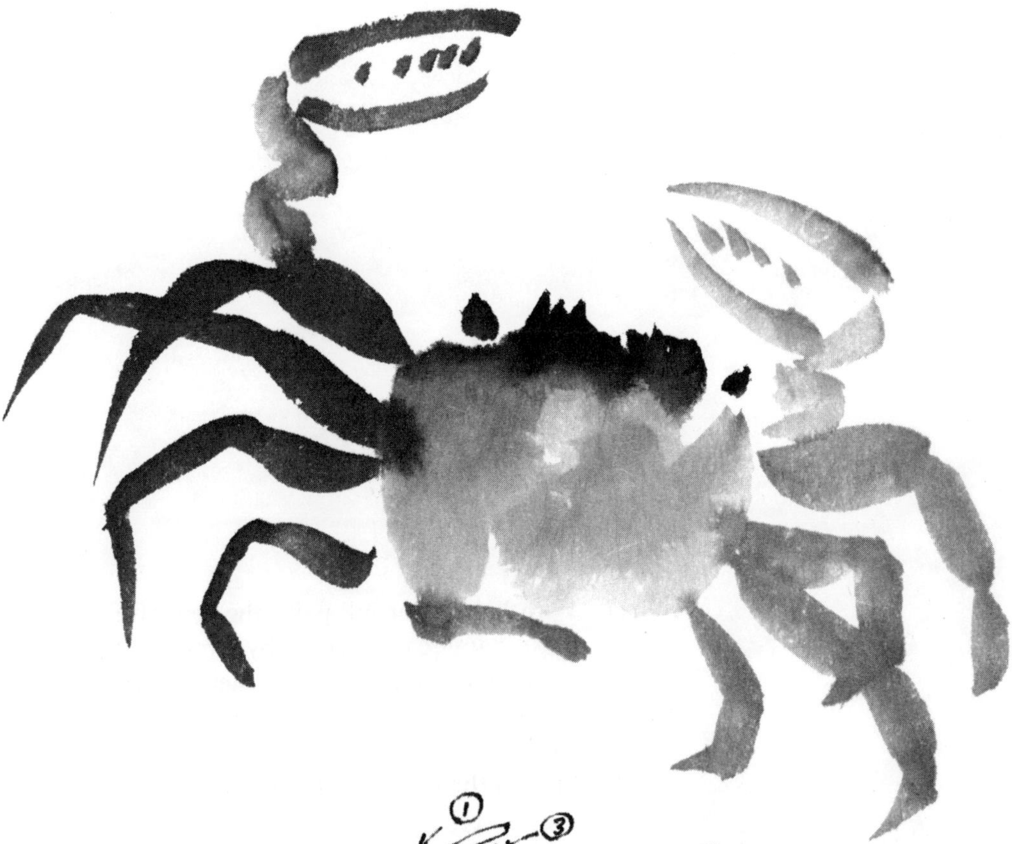

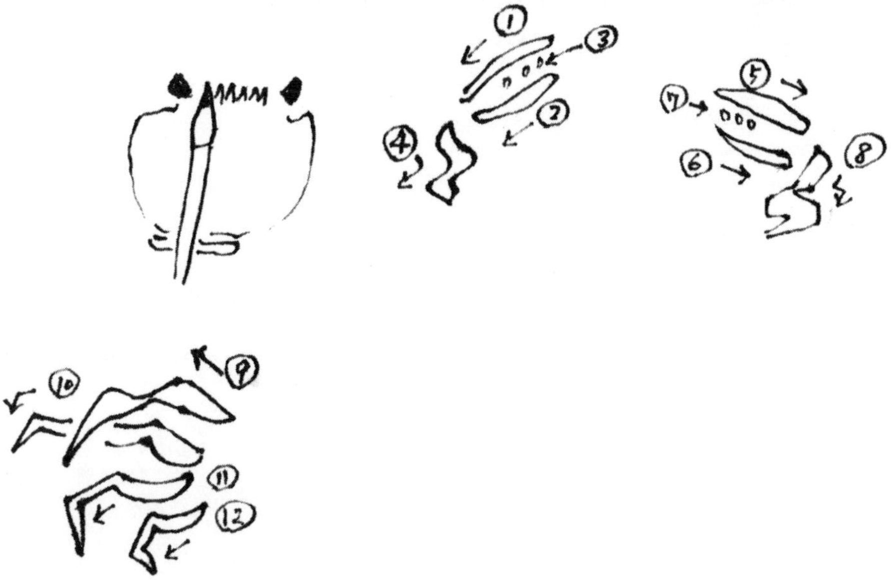

1
2
3
4
5
6
7
8
9
10
11
12

Corn

(1) With light color ink paint the general form.
(2) Next paint each kernel by pressing your brush, starting from the dark kernels getting lighter as you proceed.
(3) Add the husk.
(4) Spread the tip of your dry brush and add the ears.

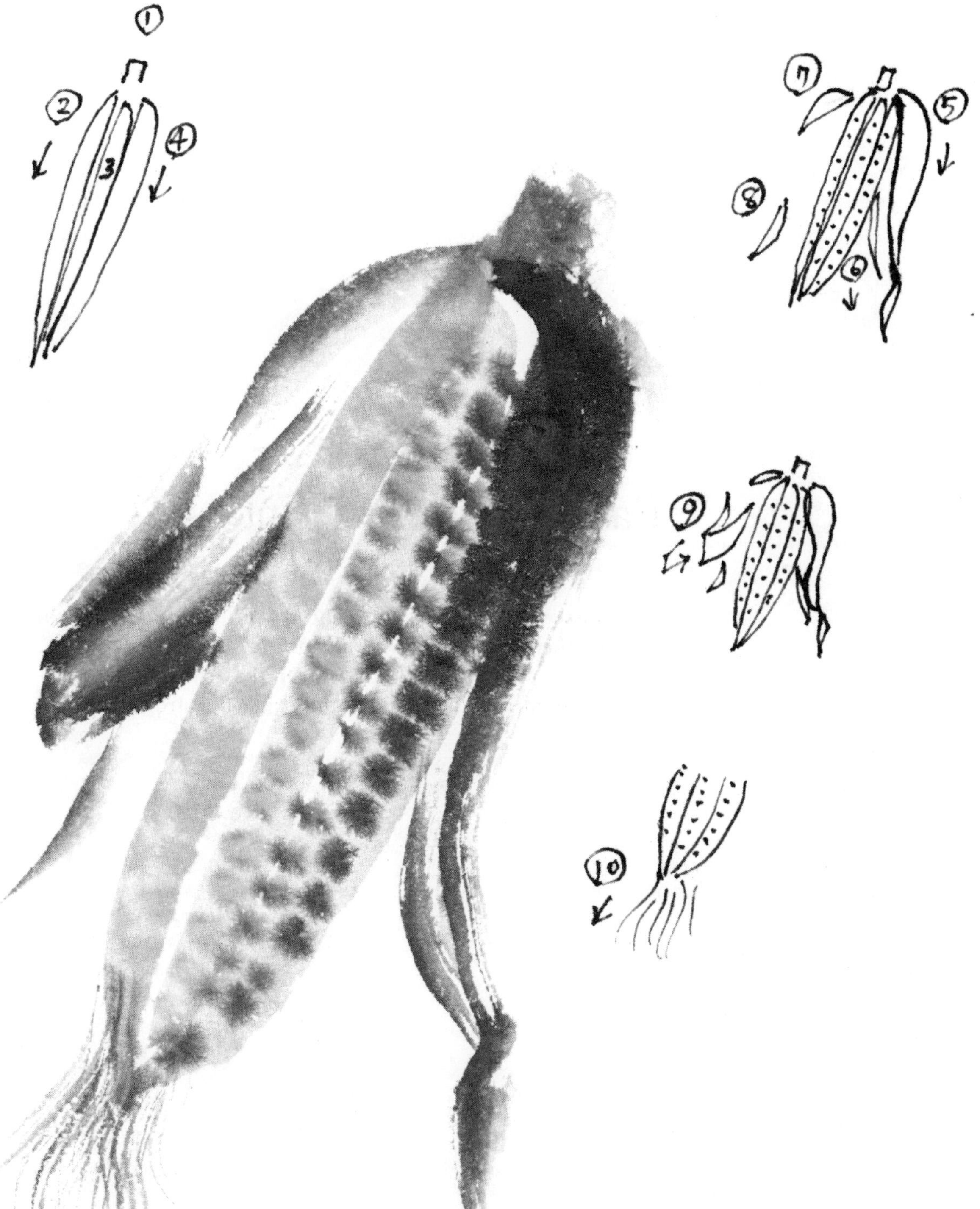

1
2
3
4
5
6
7
8
9
10

Easy Horses to Paint — I

First with medium ink paint as with examples A, B and C, then add the outlines in dark ink as in A′, B′ and C′. When painting A, B and C keep the general shape of the horse in your mind and paint it in bold strokes.

A

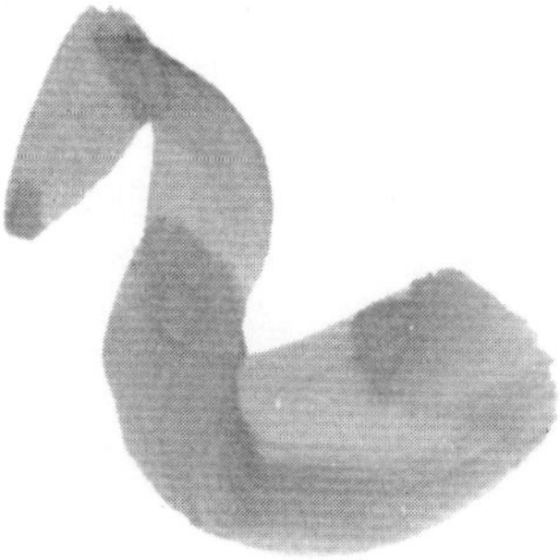

B

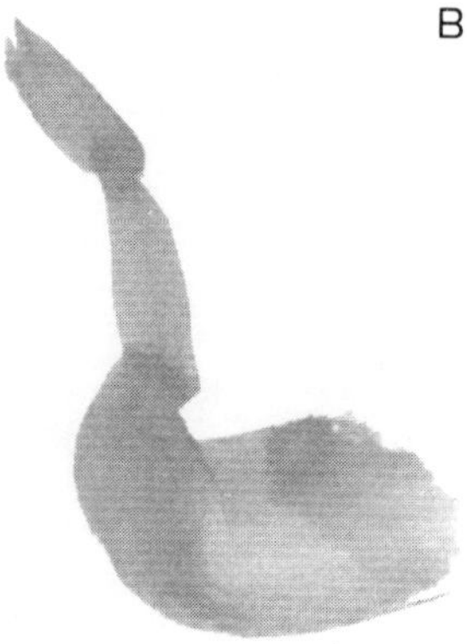

C

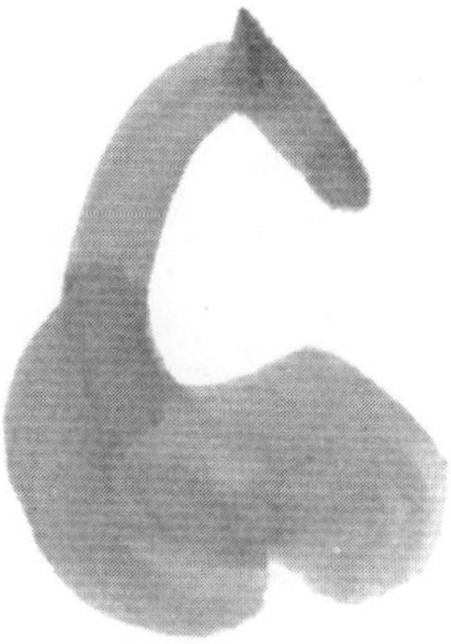

A′

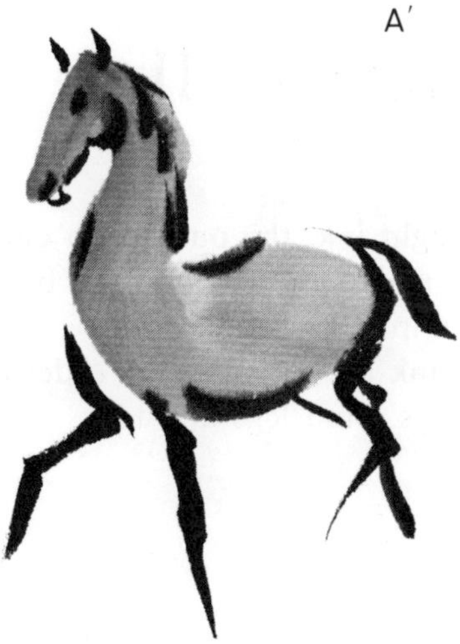

B′

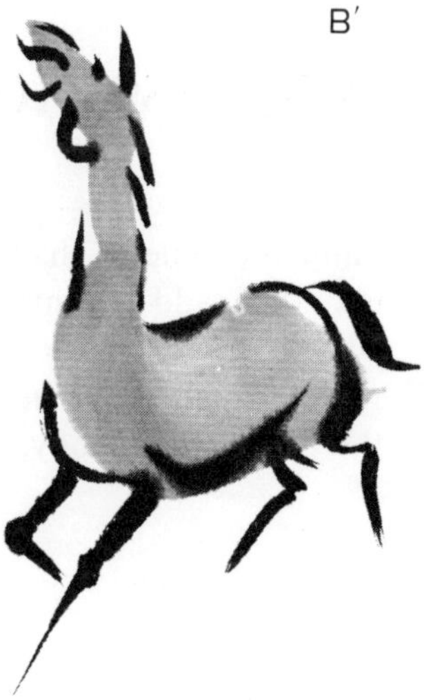

C′

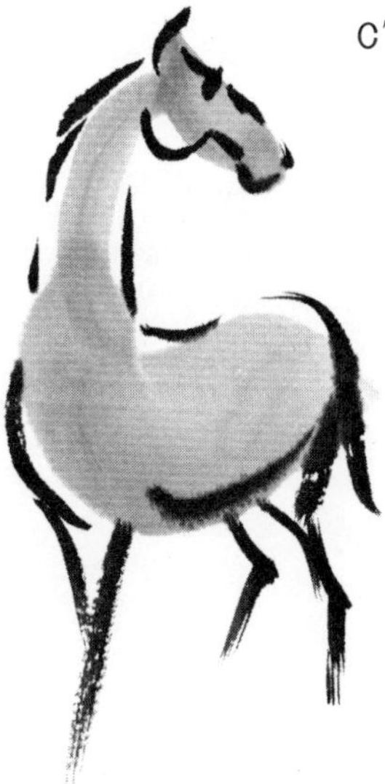

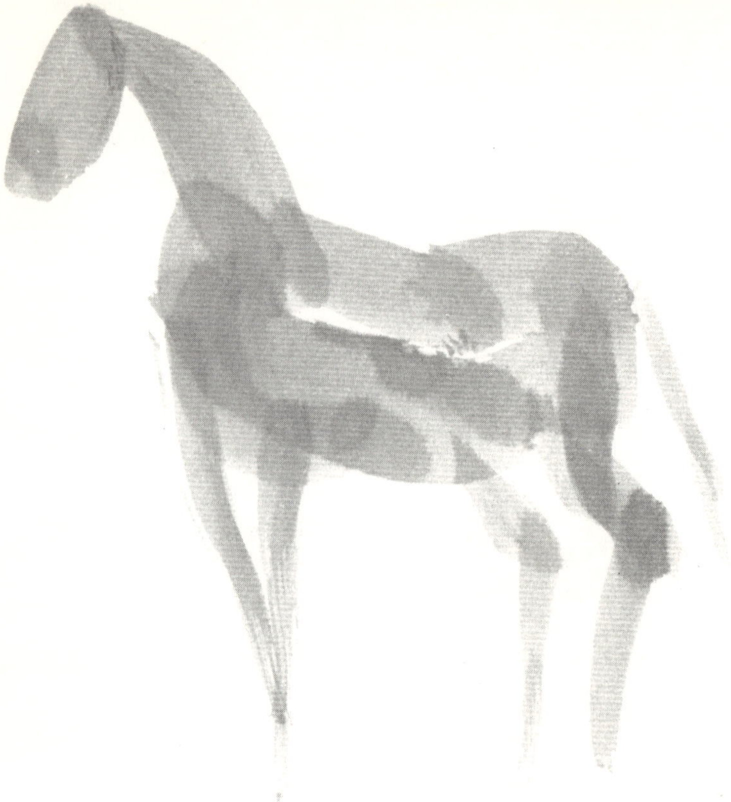

Easy Horses to Paint — II

Paint the general shape in light ink, the outlines in dark ink, then add the medium and dark tones to the body while the light ink is still damp.

The rough shape in light ink is painted in the order of the head, neck, body, forelegs, hind legs and tail.

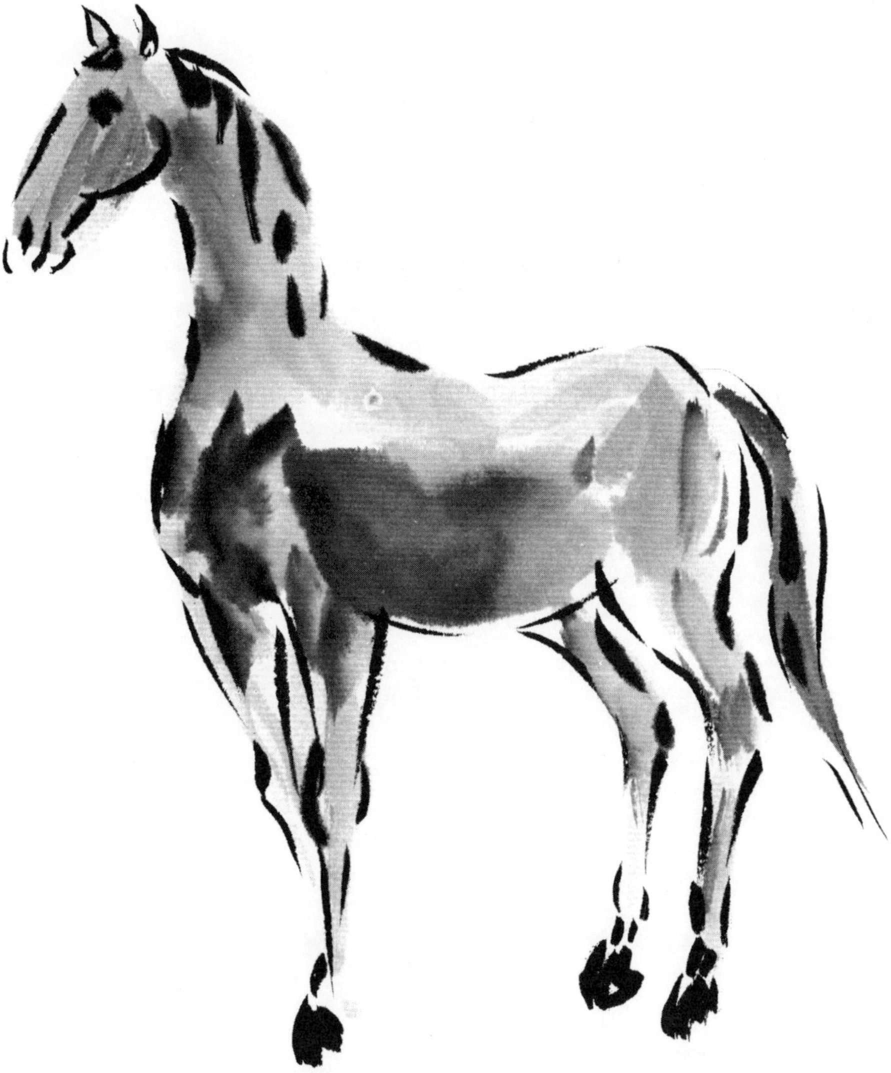

Walking Horse

Paint the general shape, including some outline, in light ink, gradually using darker tones. Study the various examples given and remember the correct movement of the four legs when walking, galloping, etc.

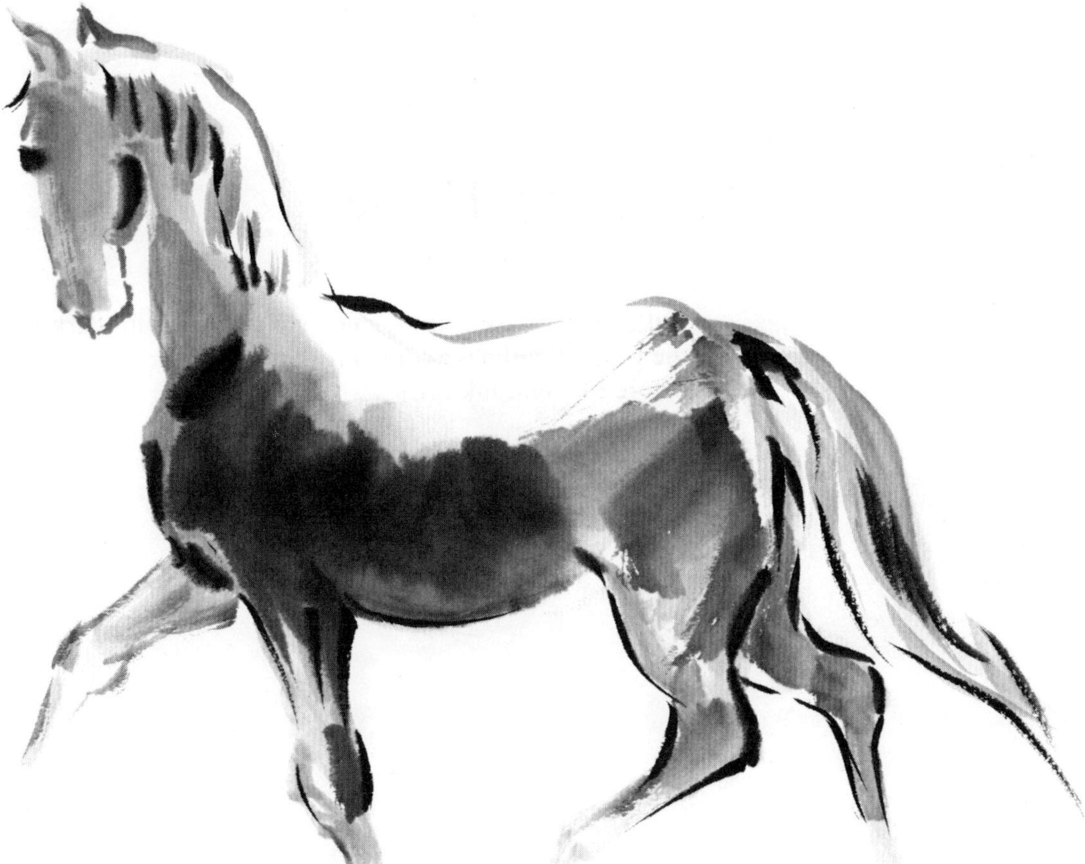

Advancing Horse

With light ink paint the general shape, then with dark ink the general outlines adding medium and dark ink touches before the light ink dries.

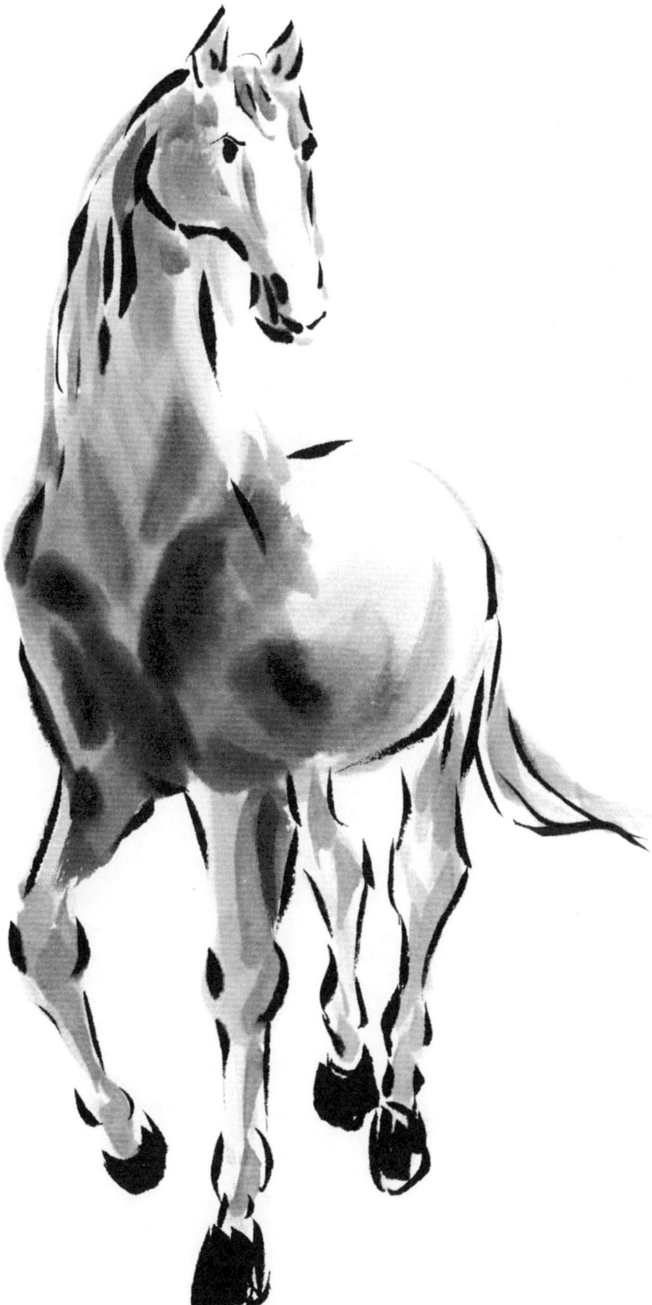

Mare and Colt

A colt's legs are very long, almost as long as those of a full-grown horse. On the other hand, its mane and tail are quite short.

This one is getting hungry!

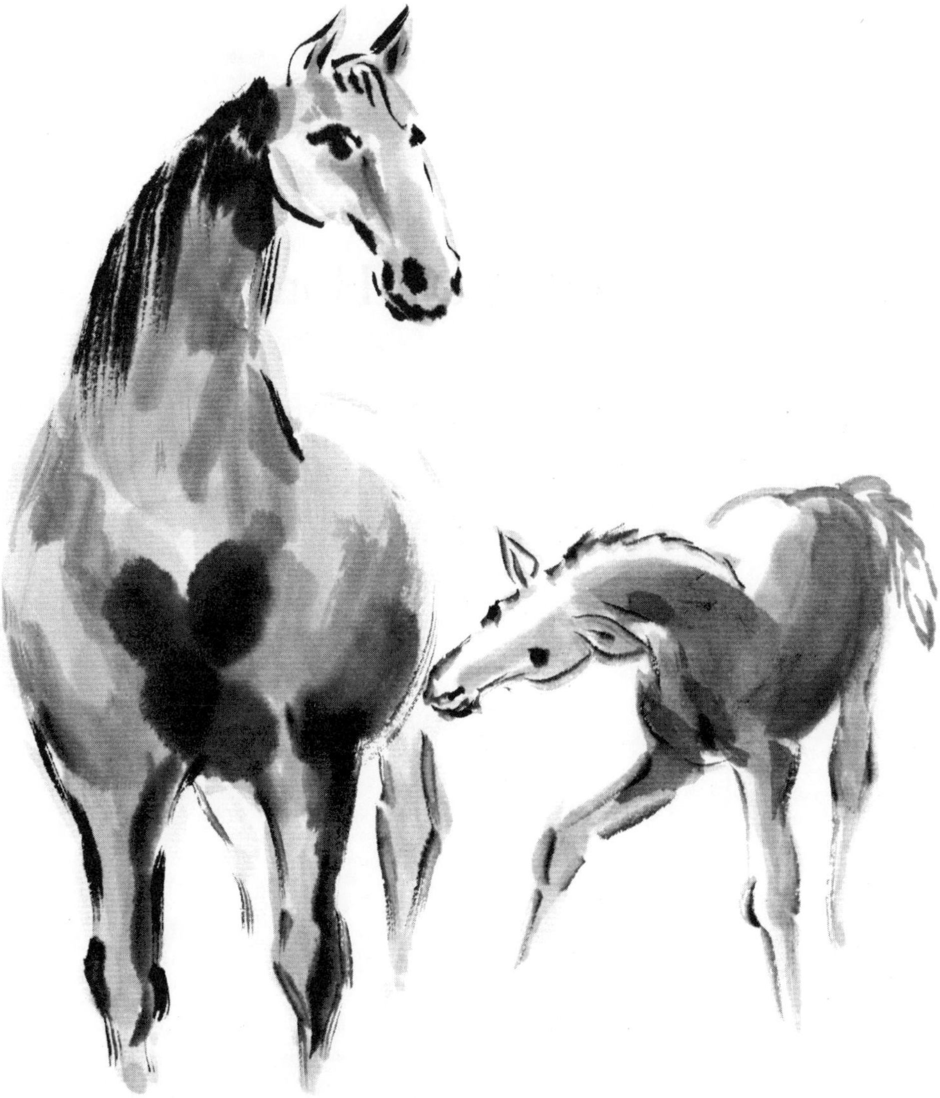

Galloping Horse

Examples to practice, first using light ink followed by dark outlines.

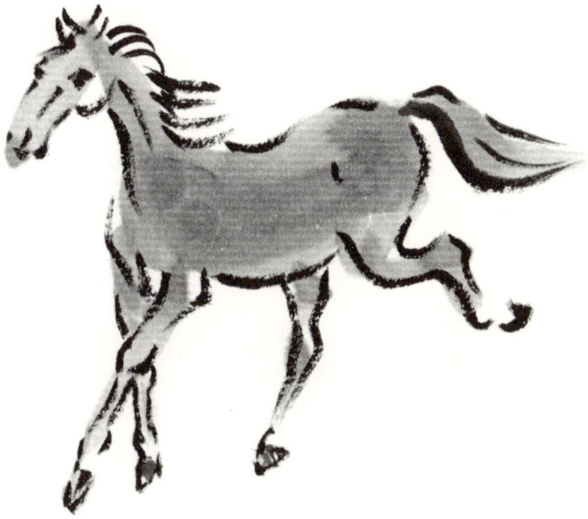
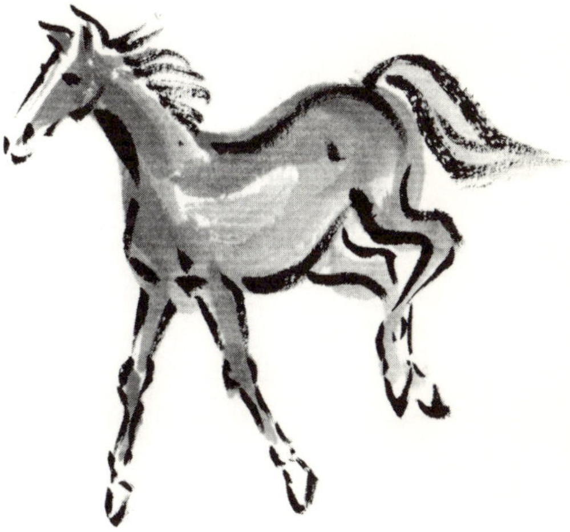
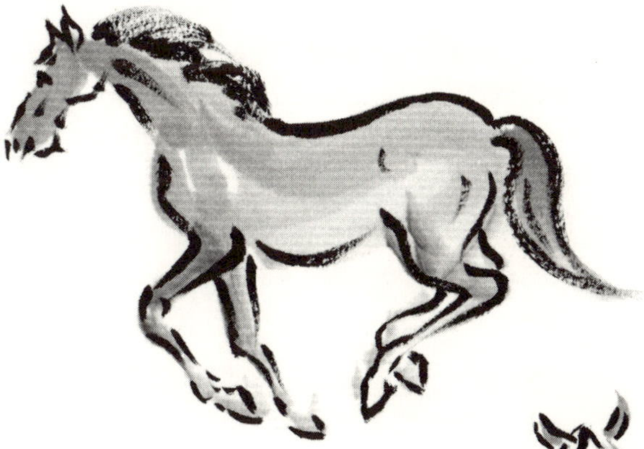
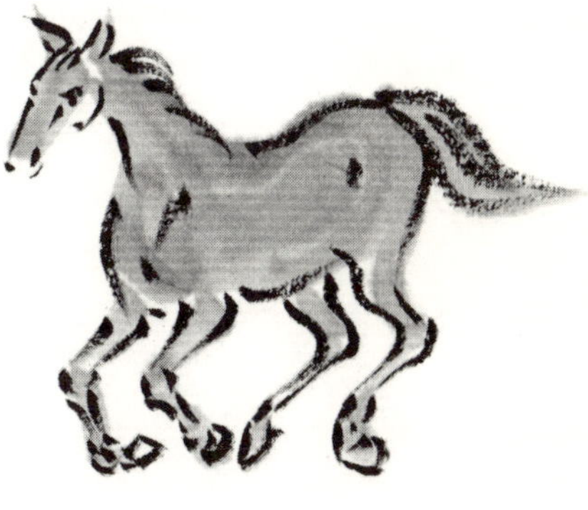
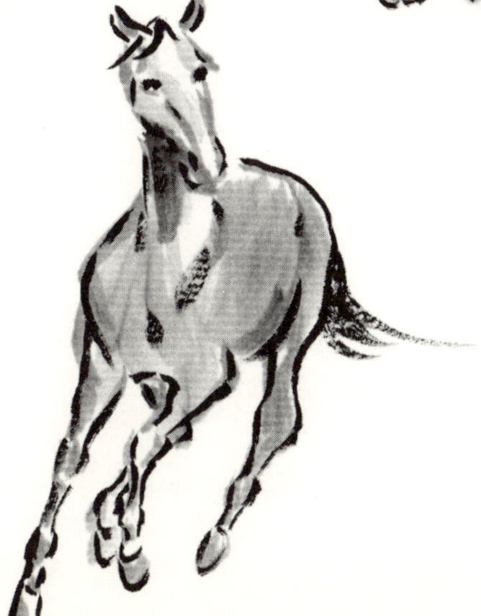

Bull

Paint the general shape in light ink, gradually using darker tones. Animals in general can be painted starting from the horns, ears and head, gradually working down to the hind legs and tail.

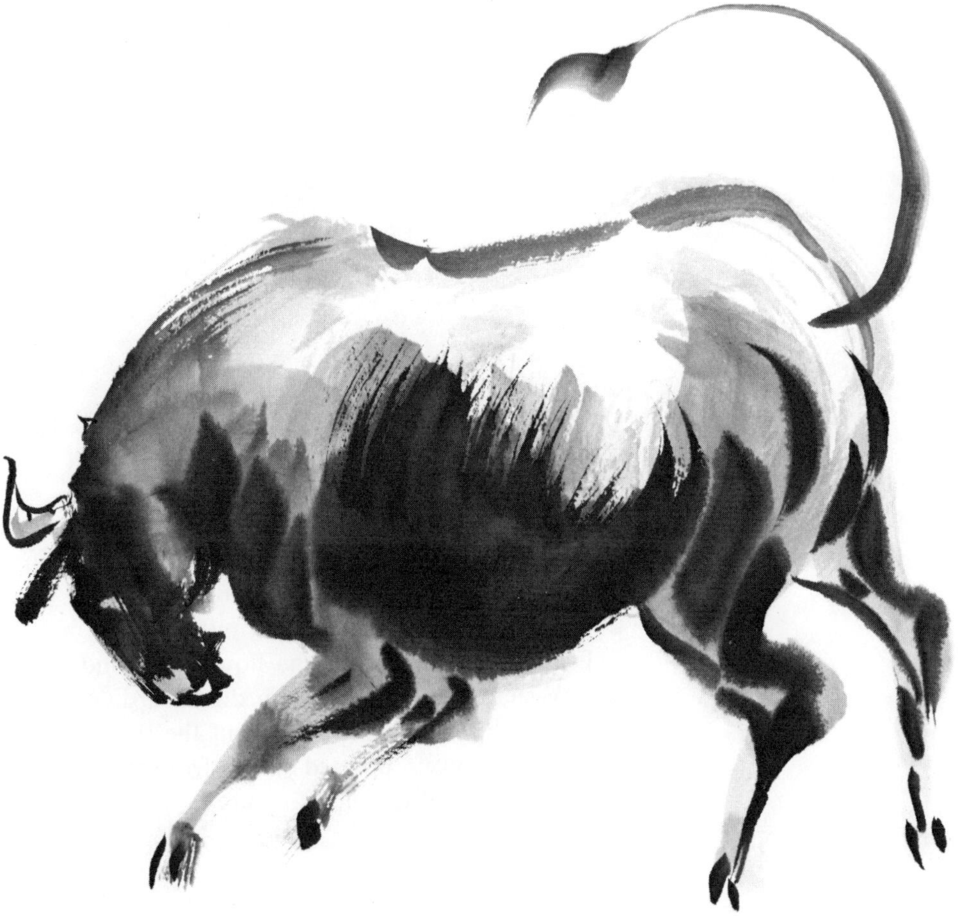

Lily

With medium color outline the six petals, add the funnel-shaped portion and its short stem, the line running down the middle of the petals and the dots, then the bud. With dark ink paint the stamens and pistil.

From the point where the flower and bud stems meet in a V-shape, extend the stem downward. Add dark ink to the tip of your brush and paint the three leaves vigorously, each in one upward stroke from the stem, starting from the top leaf down.

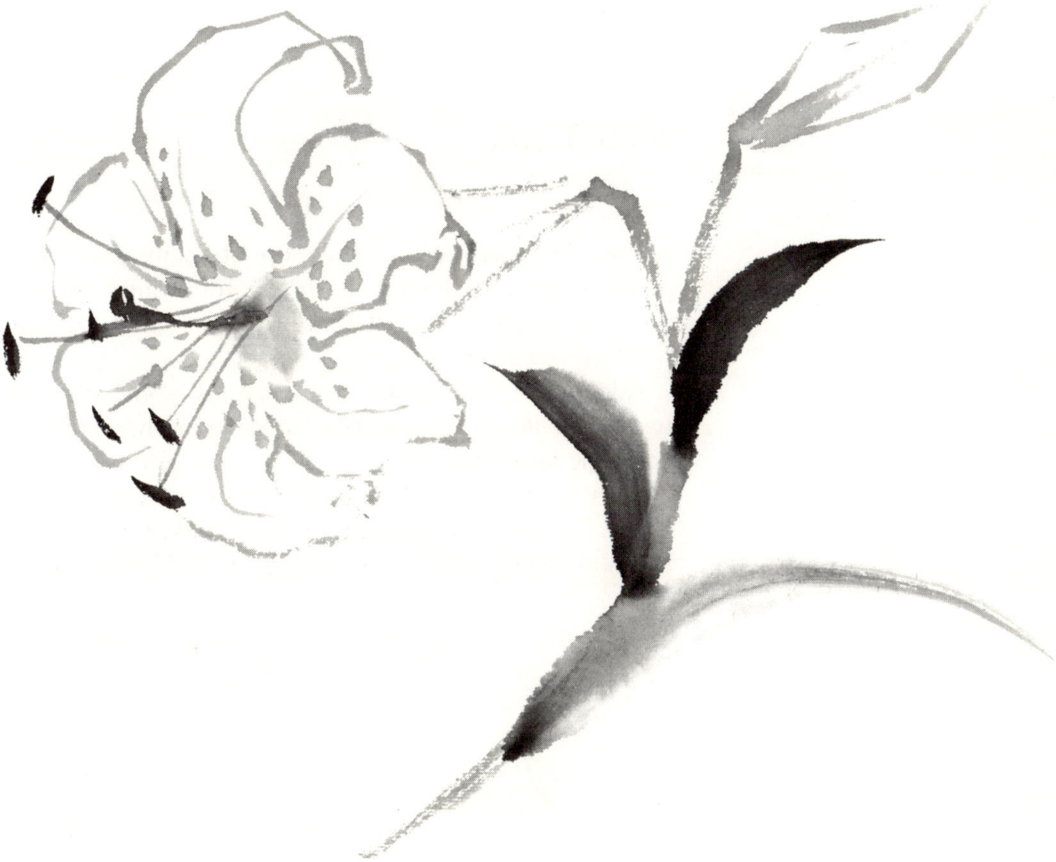

Hydrangea

As the large cluster is made up of many small four-petalled flowers, press your brush four times for each flower. Consider the gradation of tones so that the entire will have a round effect.

Add dots to the flower centers, show some stems between the flowers, draw the leaves, add the veins, and paint the large stem.

Start from the dark colored leaves gradually getting lighter. Leaves are painted in two strokes holding the brush at a slant. Paint as if joining two half-moon shapes.

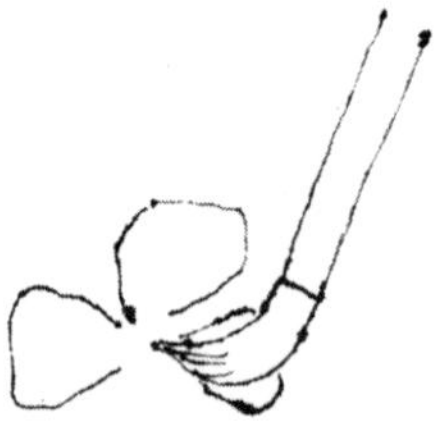

Petals

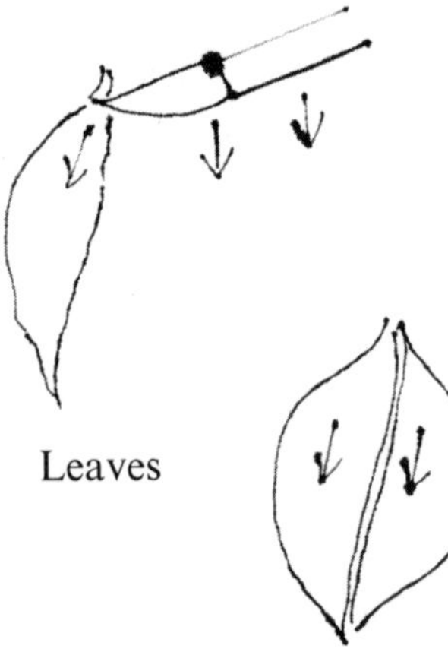

Leaves

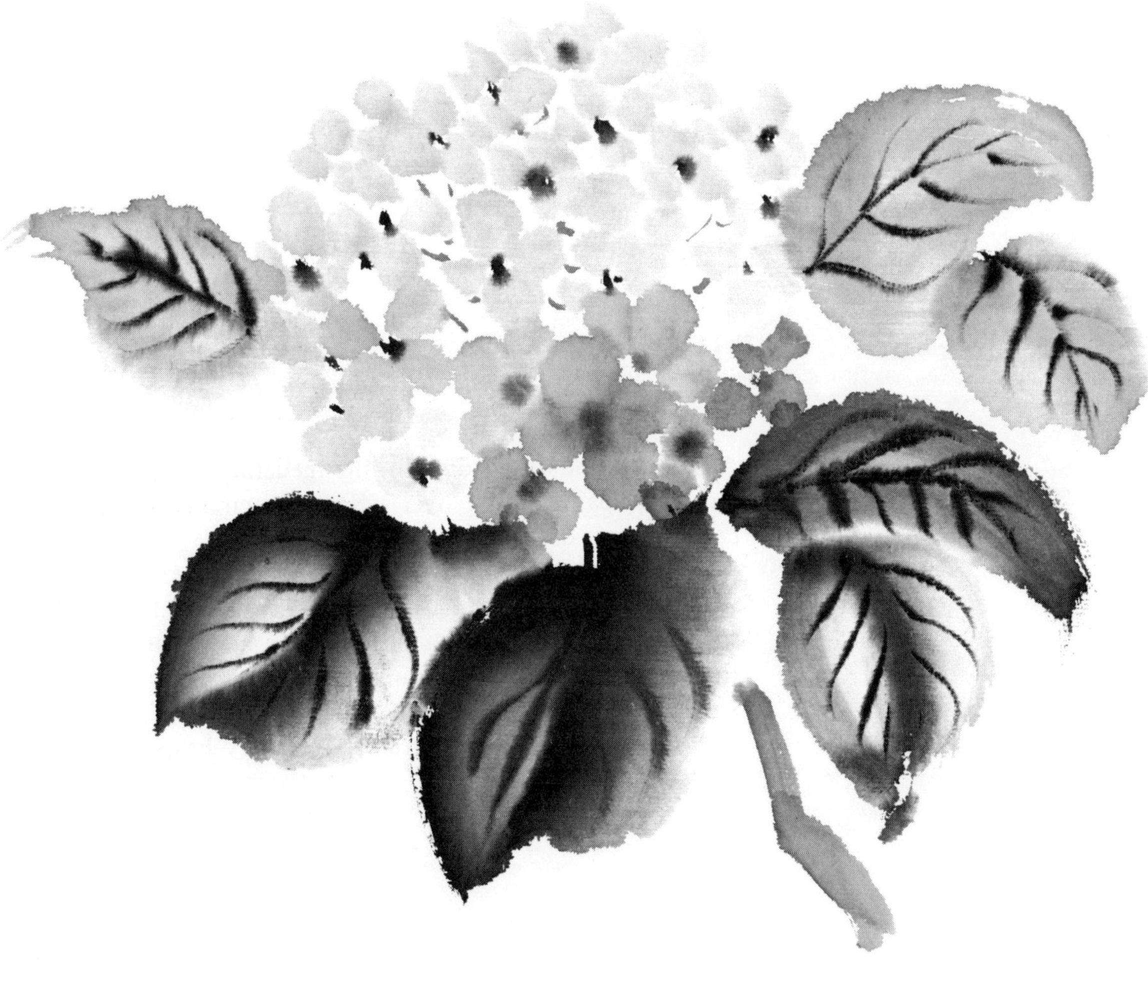

Grapes

A light foundation tone in the general shape of the cluster is painted first over which the circular form of each grape is drawn.

For the foundation, in one continuous *bokashi* stroke using light and medium tone ink, zigzag down from left to right in the general shape of the grape cluster. Over this paint each grape, adding the dark dots and stems seen between the fruit. Paint the leaves holding the brush flat, using it as in the diagram. Use a dry brush for the vines, holding it vertically.

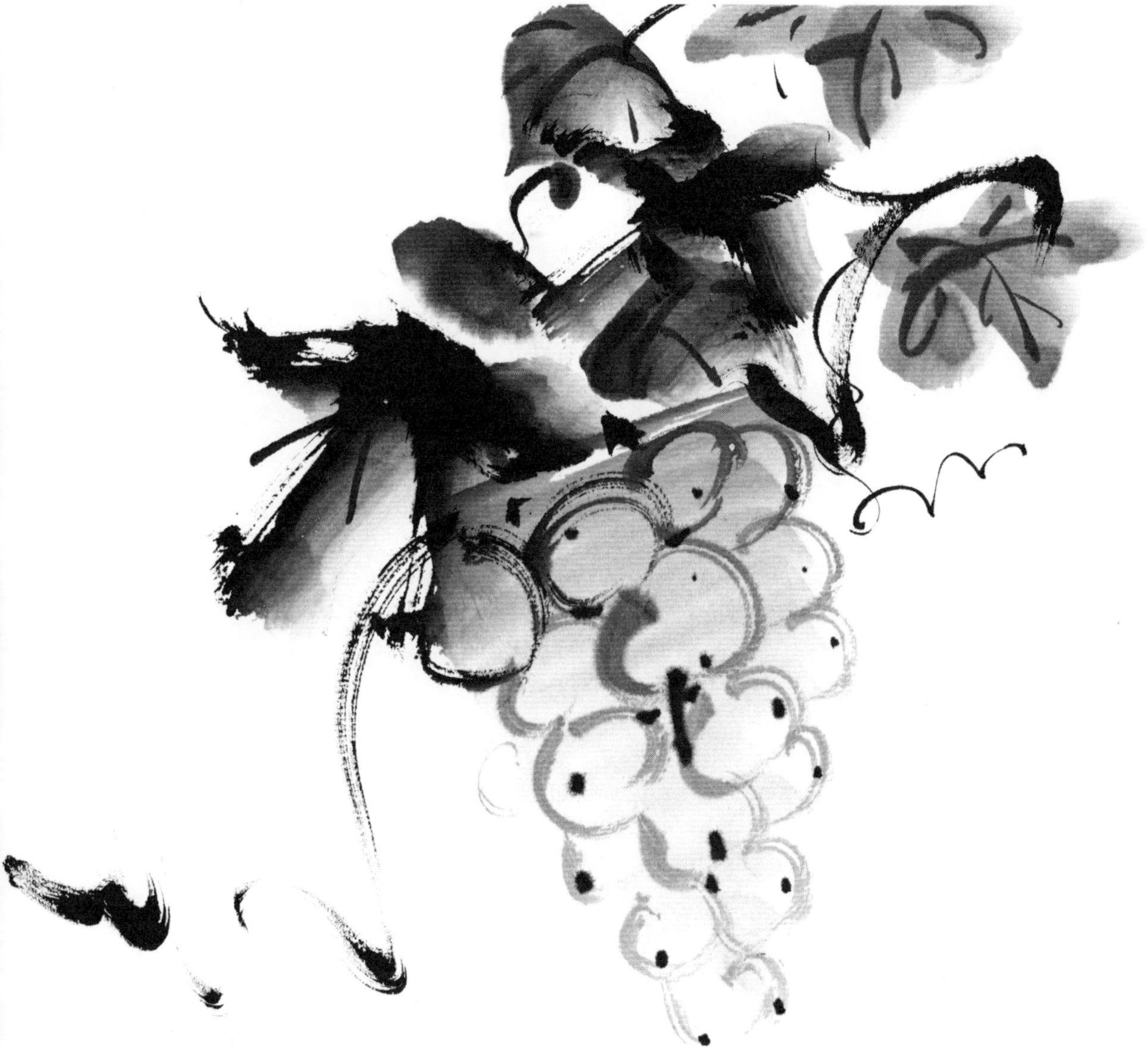

Cherry Blossoms

Outlines are used for the blossoms with leaves painted in one stroke. The order of painting is blossoms, buds, leaves and branch.

By using different tones of ink for the leaves you add rhythm to this painting.

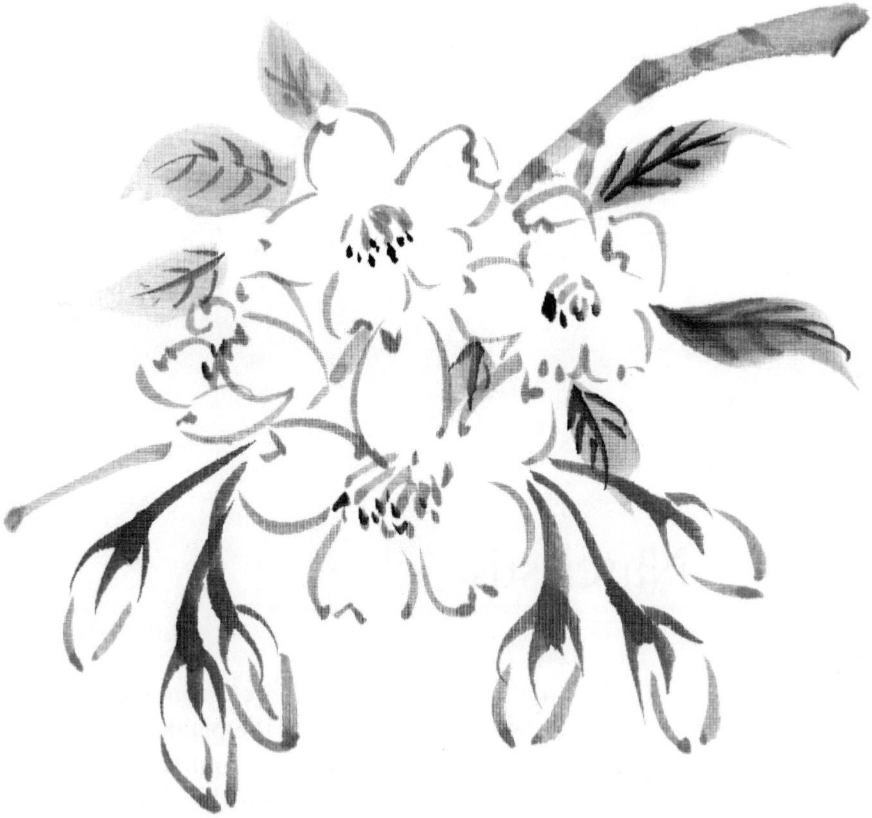

Narcissus

With light ink paint the "circle" in the center of the flower, adding the dots, then the petals with their creases. Continue on to the tube-shaped portion with the "ball" at its base, the short stem with the skin around it, then the long stem and leaves. Leaves are painted from bottom to top, from the dark colored ones to the lighter.

When you come to the twisted point in the dark leaf, lift your brush slightly then place down again.

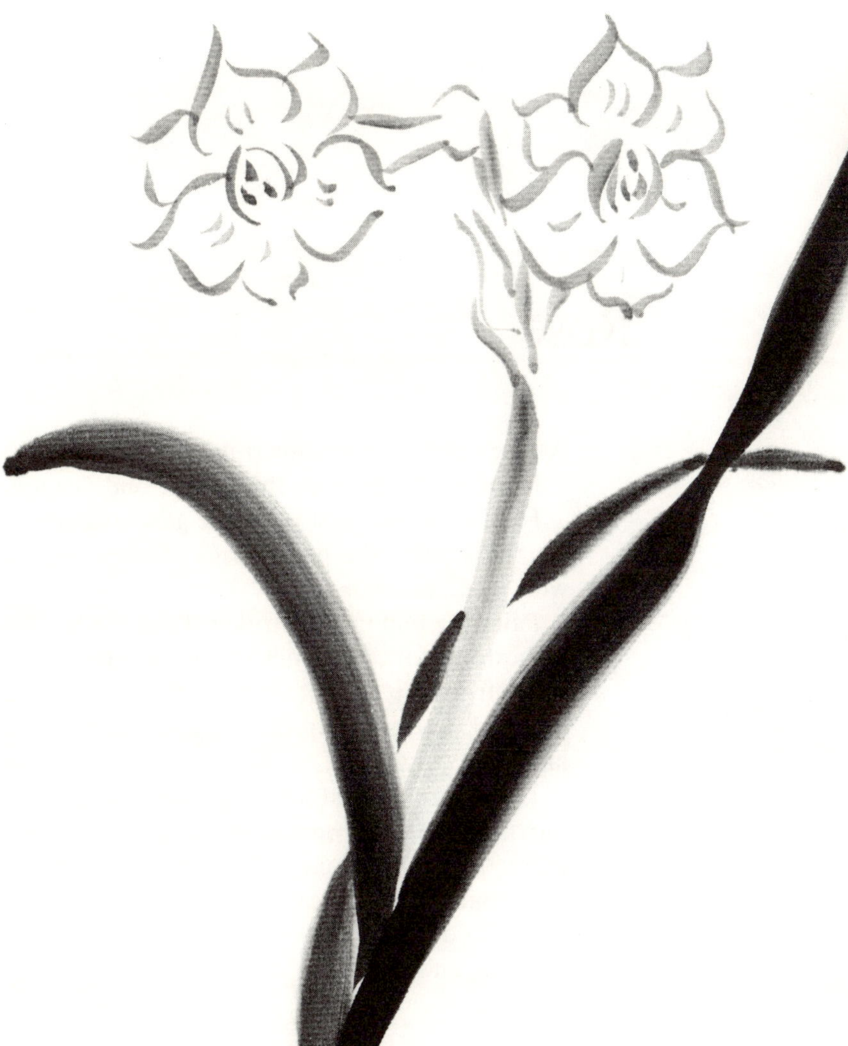

Rose

A pale pink rose is painted in black *sumi* ink.

Paint in the order of the flower, bud, leaves and stems.

For the flower, first paint the general shape in light ink, over this paint the petal forms in dark ink, add shading with medium color.

Paint the bud in two strokes. First the left side from top to bottom, followed immediately by the right side stroke again from top to bottom, joining the two together. With dark ink paint the tip of the bud and the petal outlines, lastly the calyx.

Leaves are painted from the dark colored ones gradually moving on to the lighter. Almost all of these leaves are painted in two strokes. Only the leaf seen between the three dark colored leaves is painted in one stroke. Veins added in dark ink.

Stems and thorns.

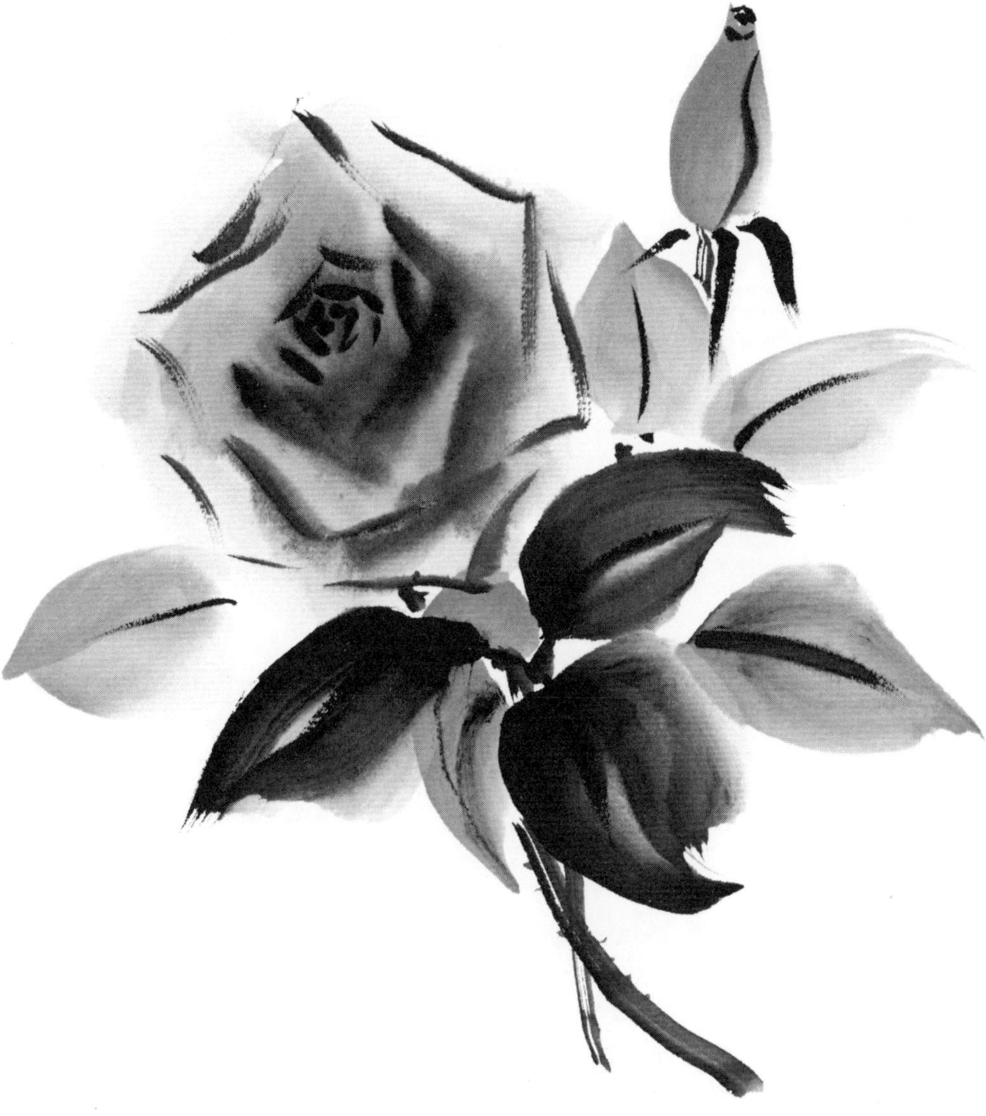

European Sketches

There is no set rule in *sumi-e* restricting you from painting this or that. It is only natural that the sumi painting of Japan, originally introduced from China and altered to suit Japanese tastes, should undergo changes along with the changes of Japan. It is nonsense to rigidly maintain that *sumi-e* "must be done in this way." True there are traditional subjects closely associated with Japanese life and nature, but that does not mean that you cannot paint any subject you wish. Art should be liberal.

In this respect, I have chosen some European scenes as examples to show you how they can be painted in *sumi* ink. These are just simple sketches and you can apply the technique to scenes of your own choice. Whether you sketch in pencil or pen, or sumi ink and brush instead, is only a matter of taste.

I find that the aged effect of *sumi* ink works well with old European structures. Try to bring out the appeal of *sumi-e* by skillfully incorporating **emphasis** and **abbreviation** in not only buildings, but also human figures, objects trees, etc.

Emphasis and Abbreviation

Take for example, a painting in which every little detail such as each roof tile or each small tree branch was painted. It would be difficult to bring out the characteristics of *sumi-e* in such a painting. Actually, there lies the real beauty of *sumi-e*. However, on the other hand, if you do nothing but abbreviate without any emphasizing, your painting will lack intensity.

There are a number of ways in which you can emphasize, such as the use of dark ink to stress the main subject, or the use of dark ink in the surroundings to make the main subject prominent by contrast, etc.

The Active and the Passive

There is an active side and a passive side (or the positive and negative sides) to a painting, i.e. the active "star role" and the passive or subordinate atmosphere backing it up. Both are necessary.

This does not mean, however, that you must always paint both main and subordinate parts.

Even within the "main character" alone there are parts differing in weight or importance, the surface and subsurface, the light and the dark . . . and whereas in one case a single chimney may be given the main role in a factory scene, in yet another, a number of chimneys may be painted to create the atmosphere of a factory zone. A chimney alone, however, would be a difficult painting to attempt.

Ink Tone and Perspective

Paintings of the old school often ignored distance. Today, however, all that is necessary is to indicate distance by using different tones of *sumi* ink.

It is only natural that closer objects are painted darker getting lighter the farther away the distance. Except in cases where you especially wish to emphasize the main subject, or the surroundings, or wish to express the weather, with landscapes in general the farther away the lighter you get.

The Rialto Bridge in Venice

This bridge is mentioned in Shakespeare's "The Merchant of Venice" giving us some idea as to its "age." As a triangular bridge is not something one comes across frequently, I always feel the urge to paint it on sight.

The foot of the bridge to the right is very dark with shadow, setting off this bridge of white marble. The approach is the landing place for gondolas, with many restaurants nearby serving excellent sea-food. I found their eel dishes superb among their specialties.

As it is prohibited by law in Venice to build houses anew or to reconstruct any portion without permission (and then only by an authorized person reconstructing identically as before), the entire city is great subject matter wherever you go, and it is a place I never tire of, no matter how often I go there.

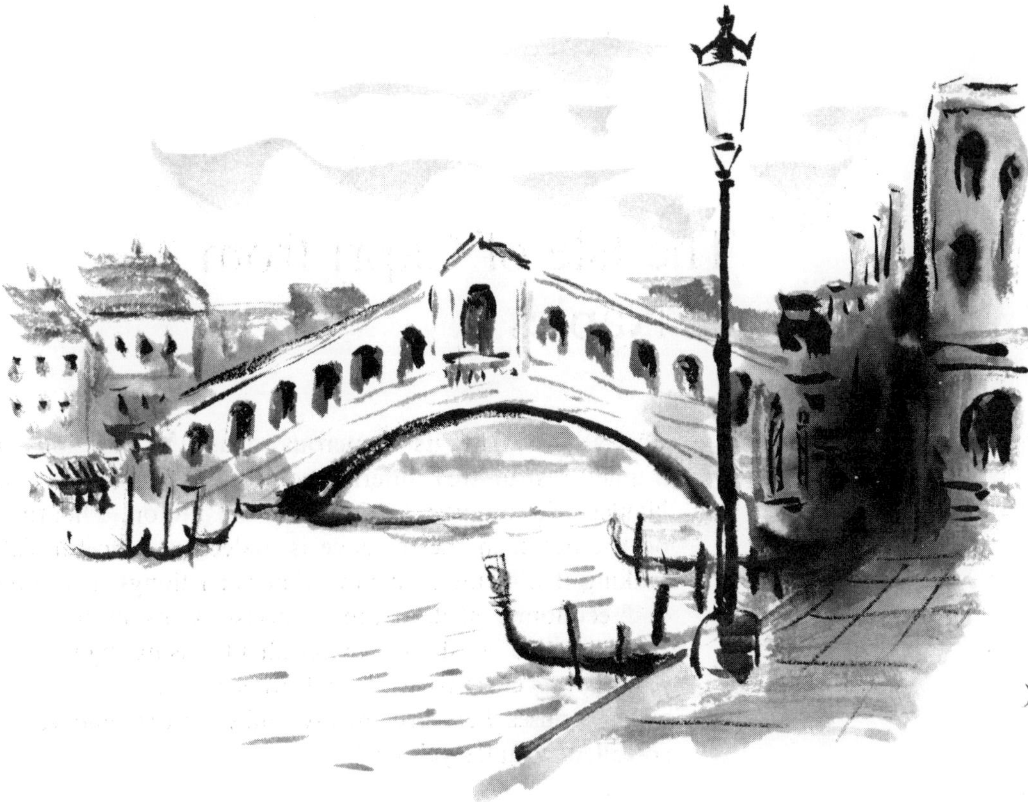

ベニスのリアルト橋

The Isle of Capri from Naples

This section with its numerous villas and mansions, is a quiet, restful area differing completely from downtown Naples. To observe Capri from the hilltop, "floating" on the ocean in the distance is, indeed, a peaceful sight making it difficult to believe that such things as politics and economy, strikes and demonstrations exist.

Perspective is shown by gradually using lighter ink from points close by to those farther away.

The houses here are mostly white or the pale yellow so-called "Naples yellow."

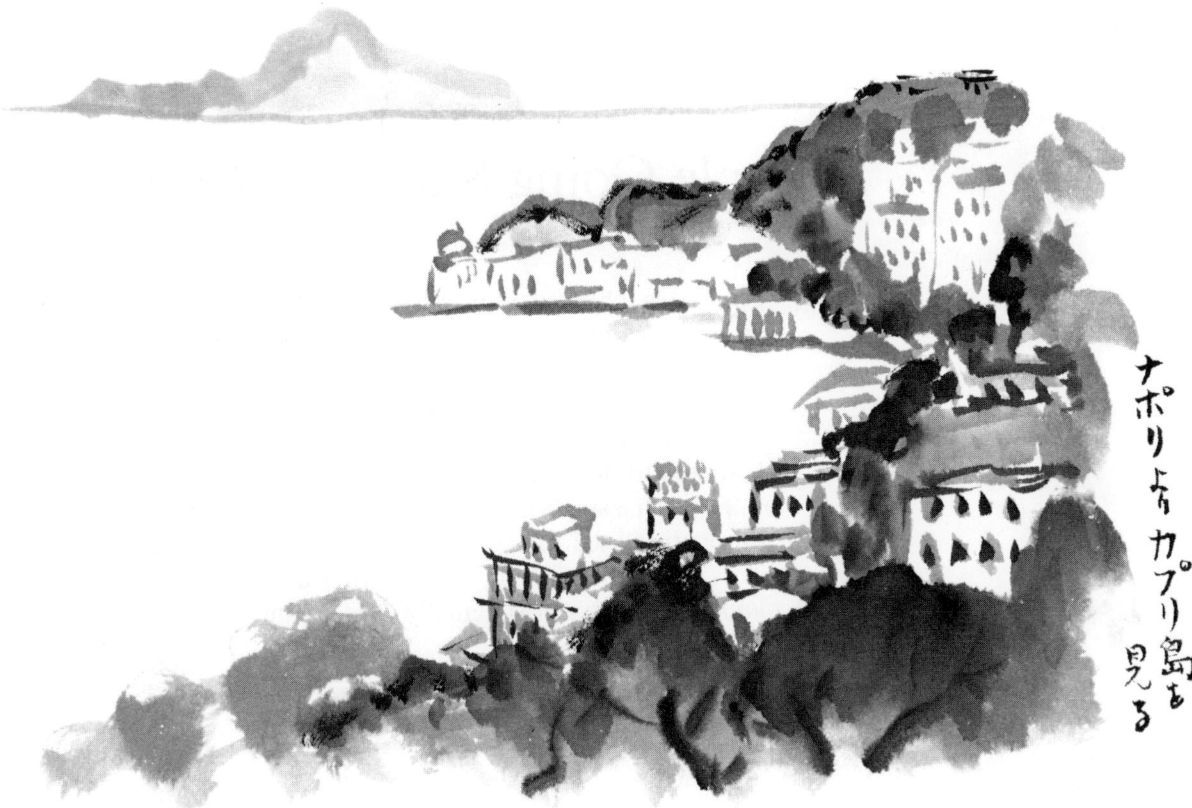
ナポリよりカプリ島を
見る

People Going Skiing — Oslo

I found a cheerful atmosphere surrounding these two, walking steadily towards a station in Oslo, Norway. Blowing on my hands numbed with cold, I sketched as I followed them around. Something about them differed from the looks of Japanese carrying skis at home and I wanted to put it down on paper.

To catch a single moment of a moving subject is nothing but getting used to the practice. Do not decide from the start that it is difficult. After trying a number of times you will find that it is actually a lot of fun.

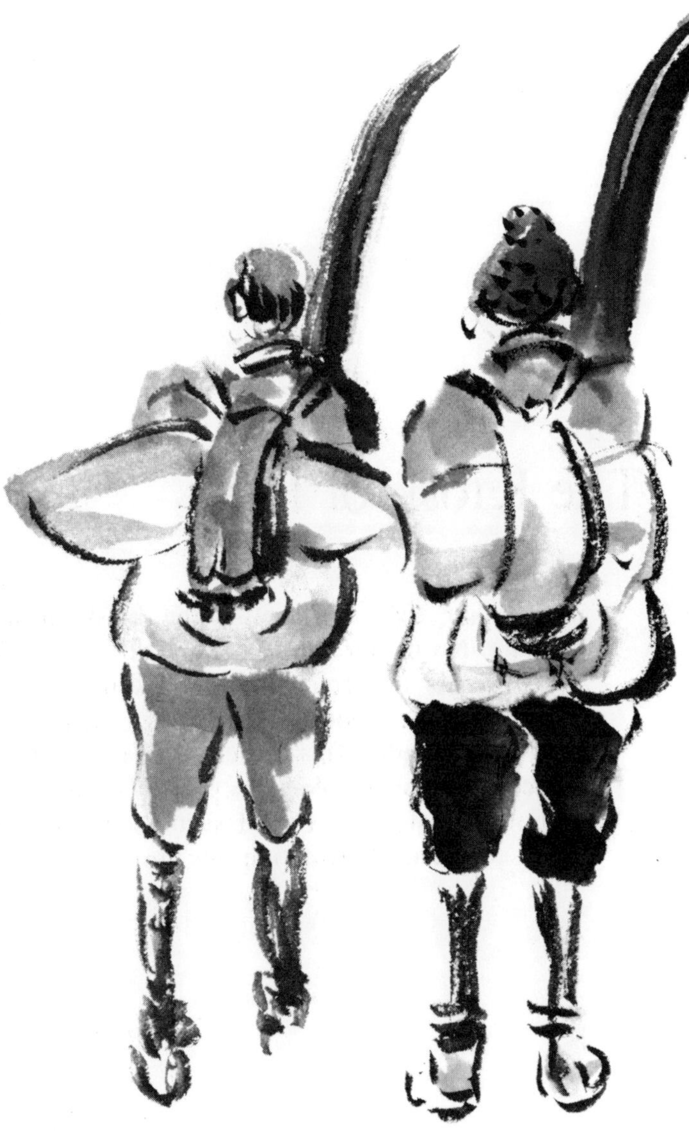

スキーに行く人
オスローにて

The Kiosk of Paris

A familiar sight in Paris is the kiosk or advertising column. No matter which way you look you will usually come across this colorful street accent. The "head" is green and the "body" is decorated with multicolored posters and ads. This sketch shows how this subject, which is a mass of color, was painted in *sumi* ink alone.

For this purpose, I used such methods as light and dark contrast, abbreviation, etc. to get the right effect.

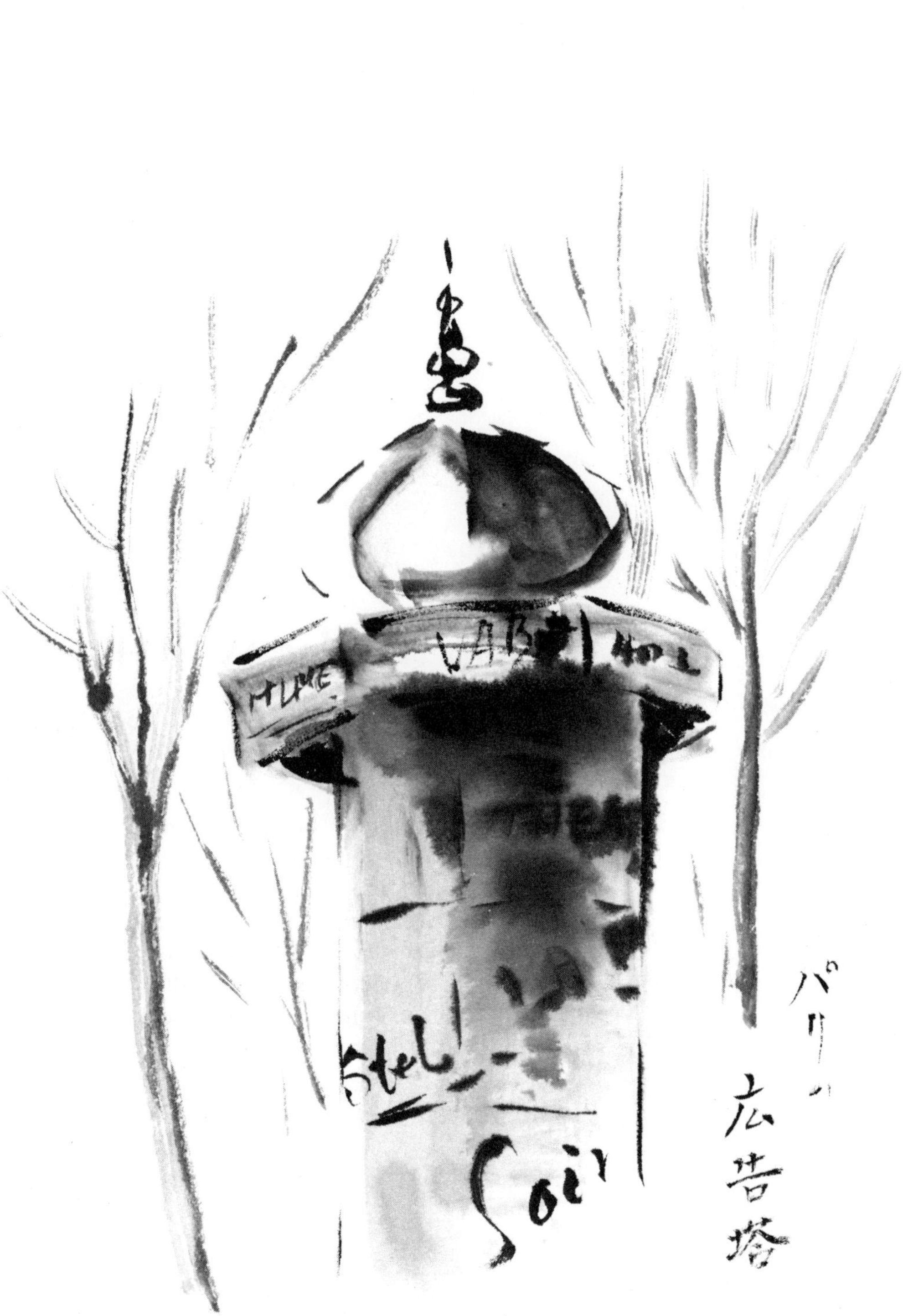
パリの広告塔
Soir

A Woman on Her Way Home from the Market — Nazaré

I found the women of Portugal to be fond of black, many dressed completely in the color, others wearing black shawls and the like. So you can see they are a "natural" as subject matter for *sumi-e*.

When I went to the fish market in Nazaré, the women shopping and bargaining there were all dressed in "their favorite color" making the place look totally black—a different kind of black market!

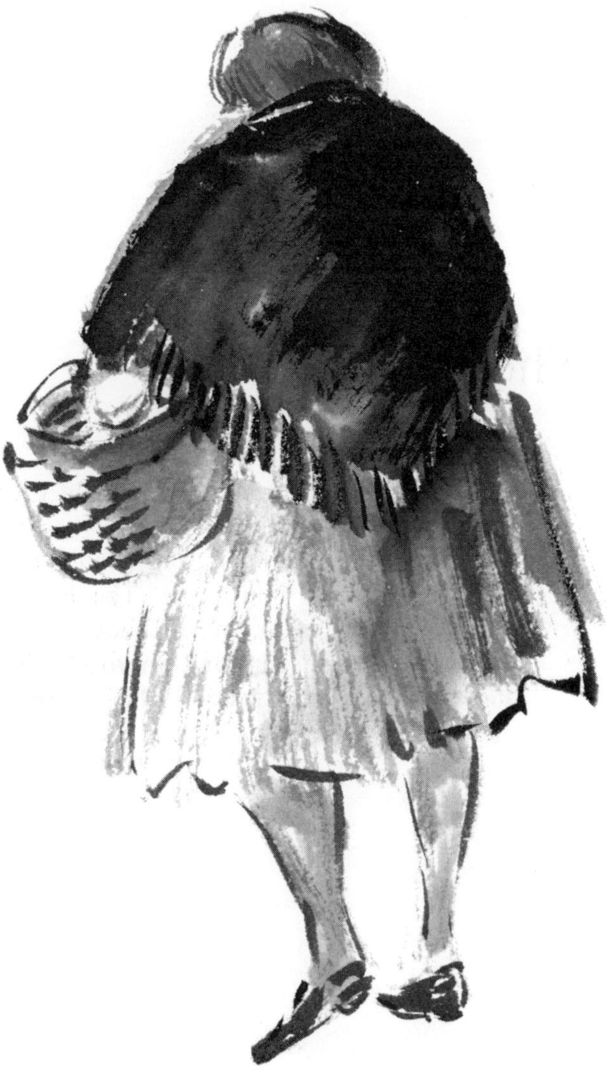

買物帰りのおばさん
ナザレにて

The Picador

I make it a point to see the bullfight every time I go to Spain. When the bullfight begins, the first to come out is the mounted picador who plants the point of his lance in the bull, injuring it. The horse is blindfolded and wears a protector over its body.

The picador lets the bull approach him from the left and lances it from horseback. It is a cruel spectacle.

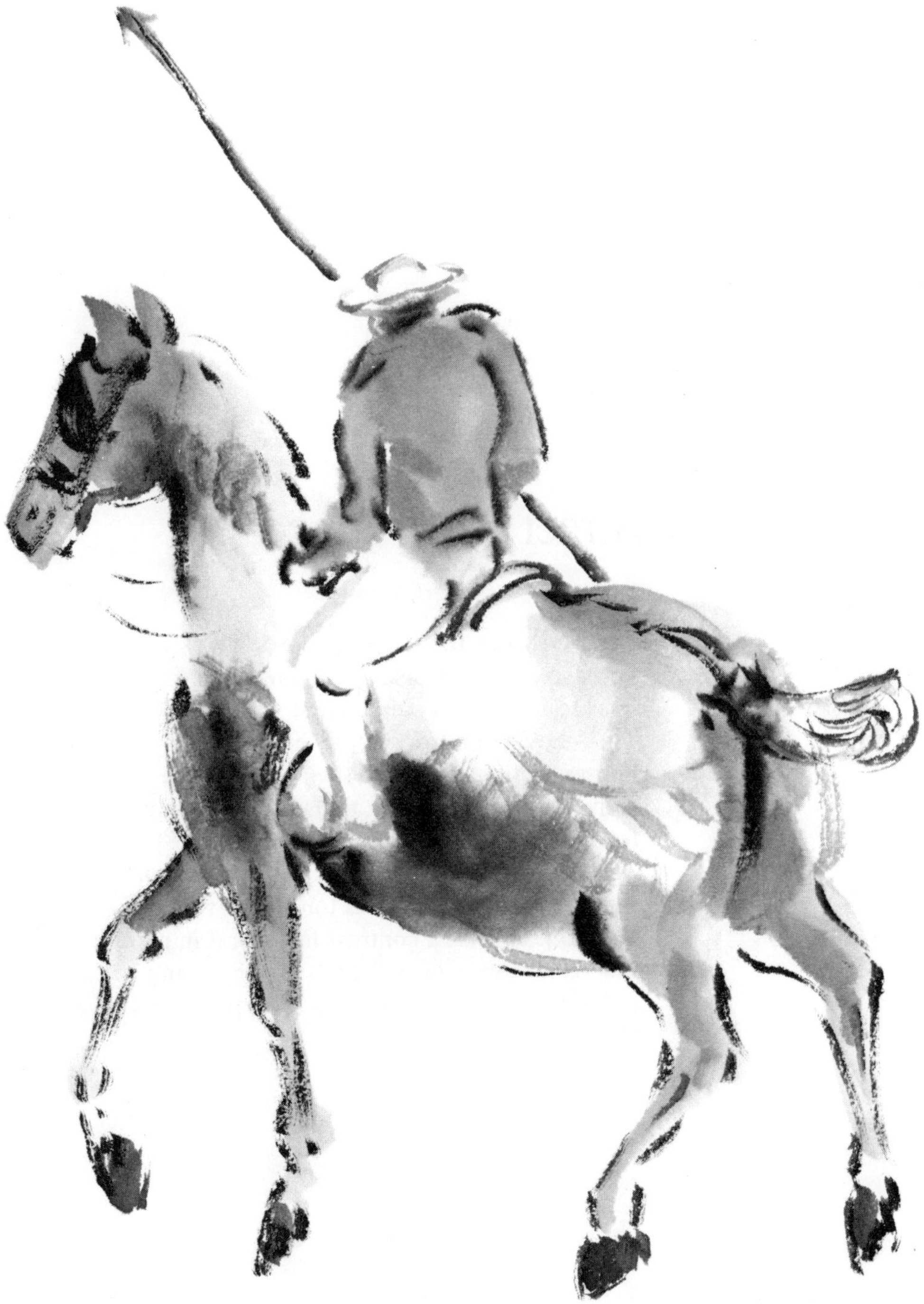

ピカドール

A Street in Monaco

I started from the left working towards the right in this street scene. The house on the far left had a highly decorative façade which I painted first with lines, mostly outlines. Then moving on towards the house on the right, the other houses were painted in their order. The center of this scene happened to be in the shade and I was able to take full advantage of my *sumi* ink there.

It is the kind of scene you could find almost anywhere, but I incorporated various tones and widths for the lines, also light and dark contrast in general in painting it. For the palm tree you will find that by using the Japanese paint brush at a slant, you can produce the effect of the palm leaves very well.

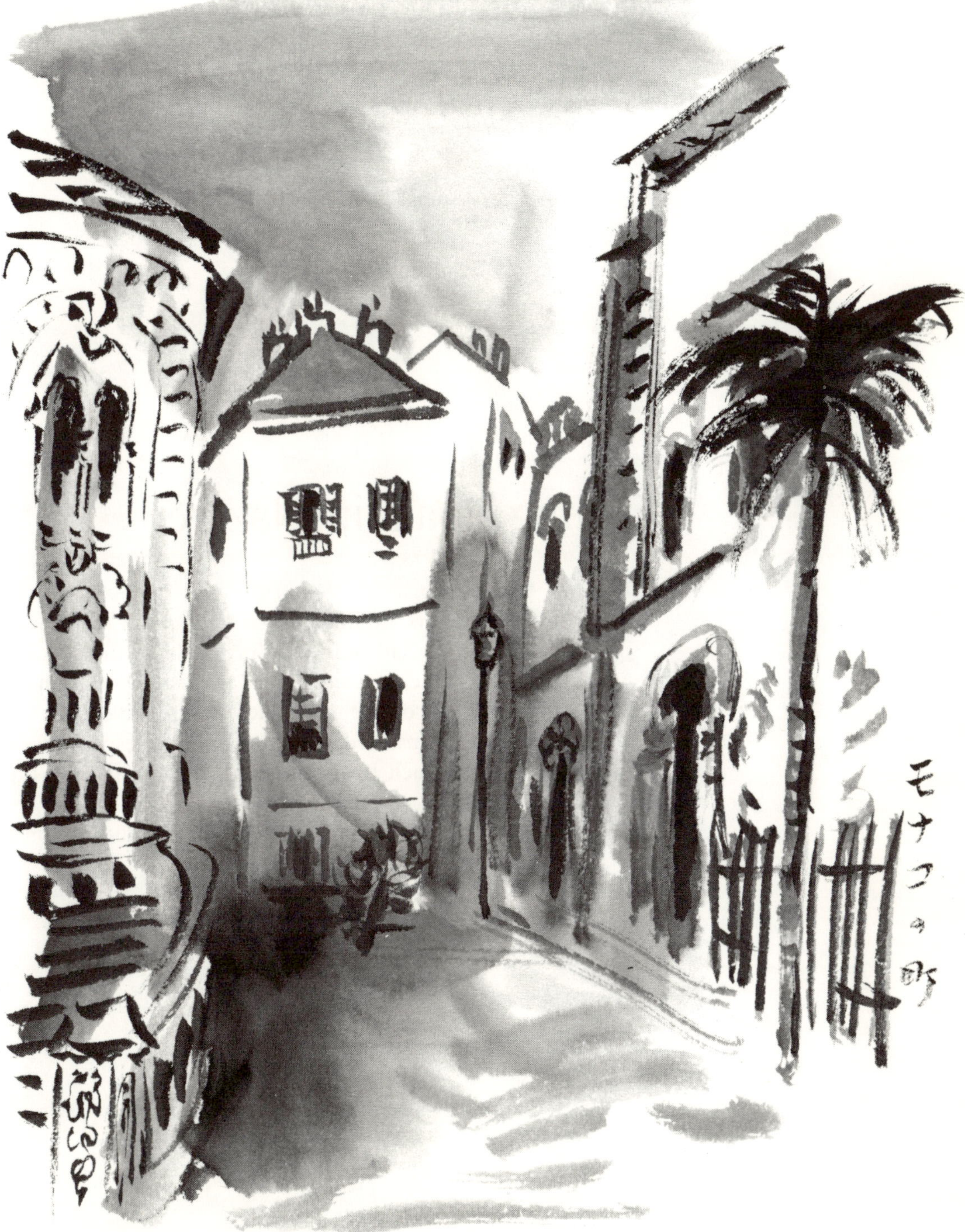
モナコの町

Fishing Boats in Nazaré

Many fishing boats are lined up on the sand at the beach. The boat with its sail hoisted is probably in the process of drying it. The characteristics of the fishing boats here are in the shape of the bow and the roundness of the hull. The hull is painted in various colors, especially in primary colors, each boat seemingly competing with the next in brightness.

The general forms were painted first in outline, then filled in for this sketch.

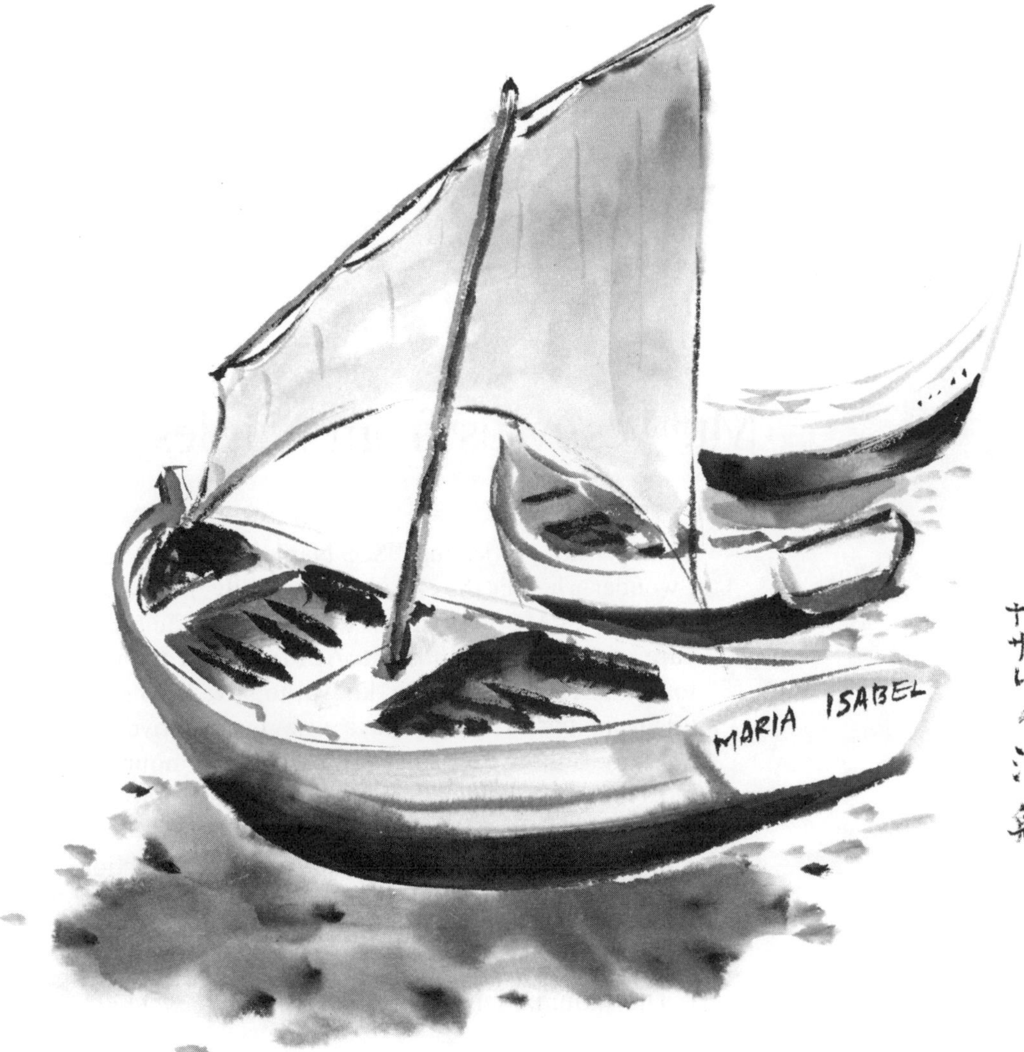

ポルトガル ナザレの漁船

Mt. Vesuvius from Naples

There is an old saying "See Naples and then die," but I wonder whether the city itself was really that picturesque. The view of Mt. Vesuvius from Naples, on the other hand, is definitely a beautiful sight. At the base of the mountain to the far right is Pompeii, known to have been swallowed up in an instant by the lava flow from above.

Many houses now line the foot of this mountain, and face the bay, giving those viewing the volcano a sort of feeling of relief.

The people who live in the residential section seen through the thicket in the foreground, probably go about their lives looking at this beautiful view all the year round.

The mountain is painted here in light *sumi* ink.

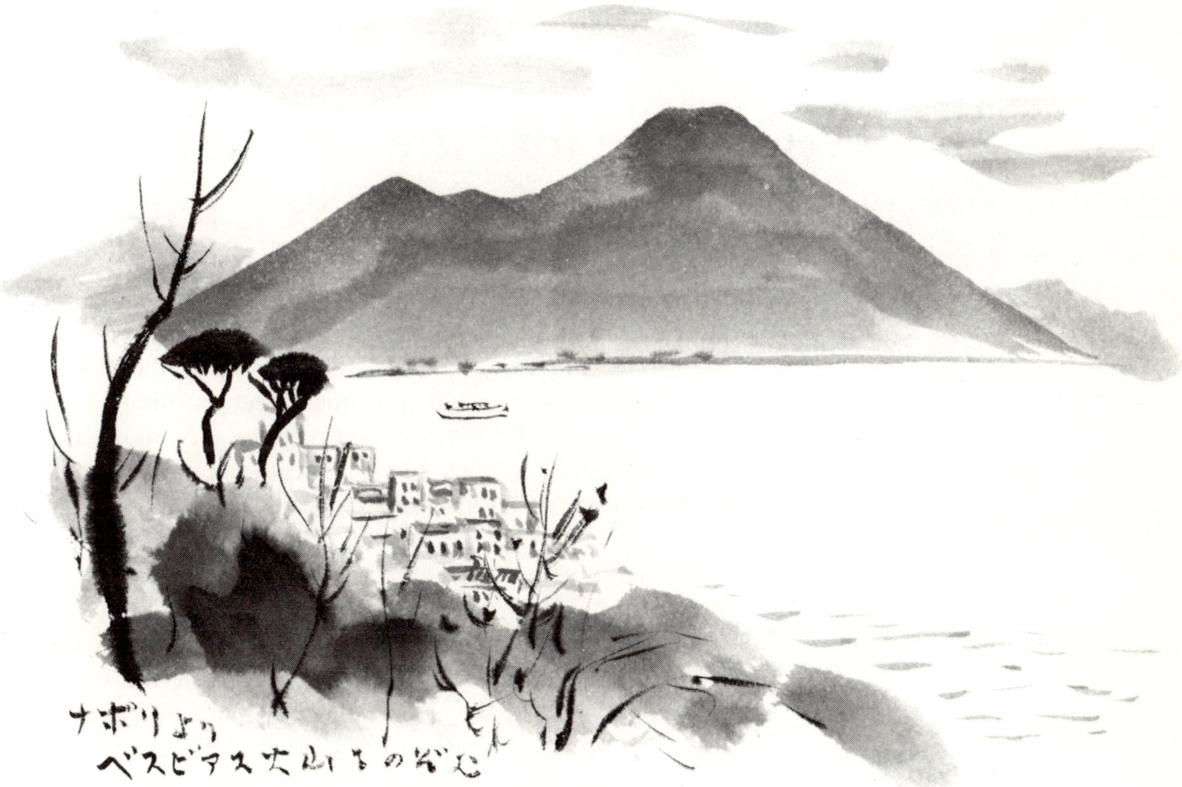
ナポリより
ベスビアス火山をのぞむ

Carriage for Hire—Rond-Point des Champs-Élysées, Paris

Down the Avenue des Champs-Élysées, halfway between the Étoile and the Place de la Concorde, is the Rond-Point. Avenues from all directions meet at this "round point," one of the main rotaries of the city. It is also a starting point from where people scatter in all directions, and horse carriages for tourists are waiting here to be hired.

To me, carriages are precious accents to cities and towns, and I am happy that there are still many to be found in use in Europe. Even in America, the Amish still use carriages instead of cars. In the northeastern districts of Japan in winter, the horse-sleigh plays an active part in the snow. When in southern Italy, I charter a carriage to go sketching. I find the height of the carriage and the pace of the horse most convenient for my purpose.

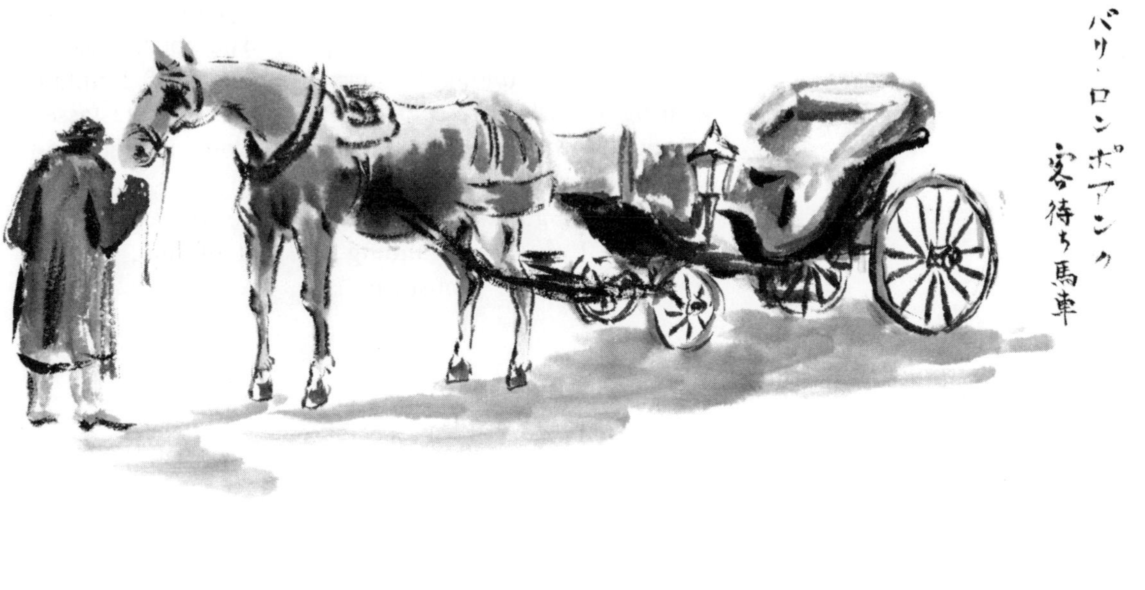
バリ・ロンポアンの
客待ち馬車

The Queen's Life Guard — London

The barracks in London can be found in town situated rather casually among banks, shops and government offices. Their not being particularly conspicuous, one sometimes unexpectedly comes upon a guard standing at attention while walking about town. The appearance of a Life Guard among the gray buildings of London, wearing a scarlet overcoat and helmet with white tassel, mounted with stern face and drawn sword, is indeed an attractive sight.

This quiet guard at Whitehall, made not a move all the while I sketched standing in front of him, a most convenient subject I must say.

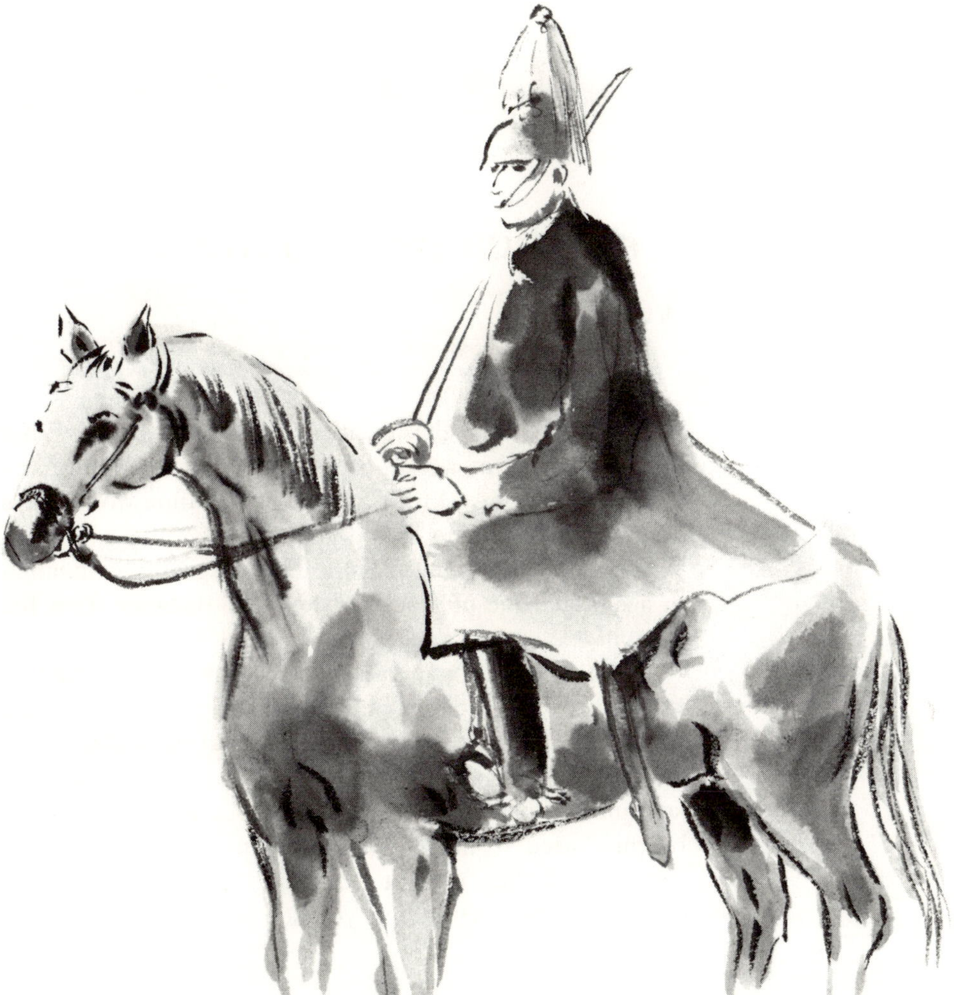

ロンドン
女王近衛騎兵

The Basilica della Salute, Venice

Towards evening, the Basilica della Salute shows her form distinctly in a beautiful silhouette. I should think that anyone in St. Mark's Square at this time would have his eyes fixed on this grand sight.

The wooden landing place in the foreground is painted in a darker tone of black to show the distance from the church.

Lines, dots and flat areas have been naturally combined very well in this composition, this same church in the morning haze also being a most beautiful sight.

The poles around the landing are for mooring gondolas, and in treeless Venice are precious things that must be purchased from afar. When painting these poles be careful that they do not "become" iron bars, painting each one while reminding yourself that it is wooden.

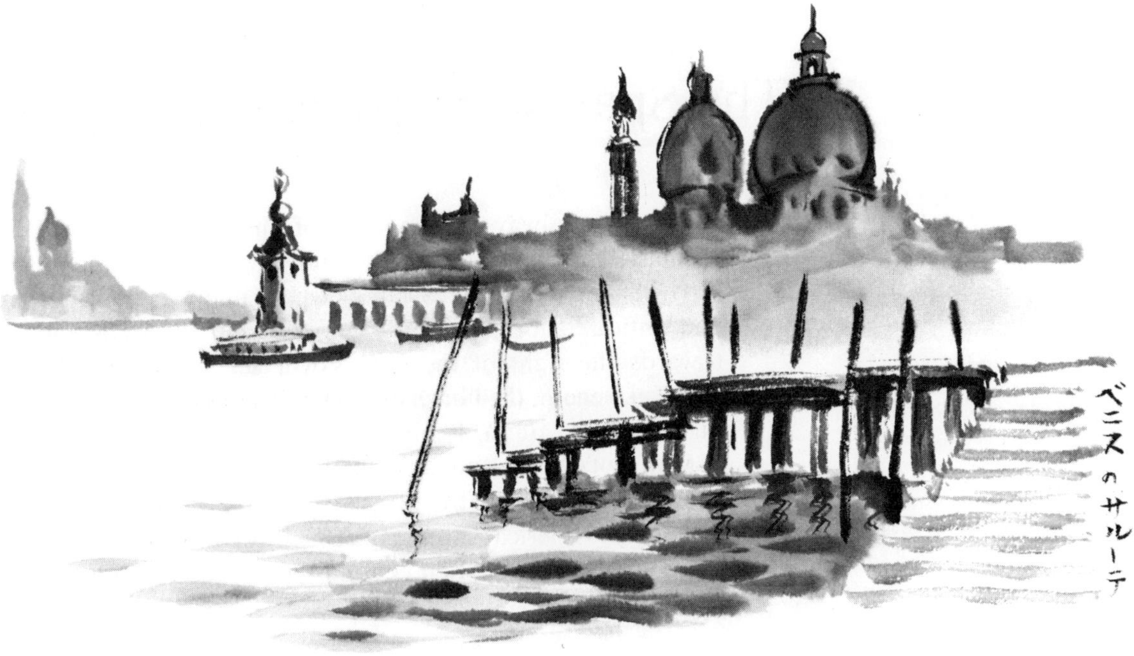
ベニスのサルーテ

The Spanish Steps, Rome

These steps always remind me of the movie "Roman Holiday" in which they were shown.

To the left of the steps can be found many art galleries and antique shops, one after another. Up the steps and towards the right of the towers will get you to the Via Vittorio Veneto, the Ginza of Rome. The towers are those of the Chiesa de la Trinità dei Monti.

Many of the apartments on the left hand side of the steps are occupied by artists from other countries—especially America—and, consequently, models hoping to be hired can very often be found in numbers wandering about these steps.

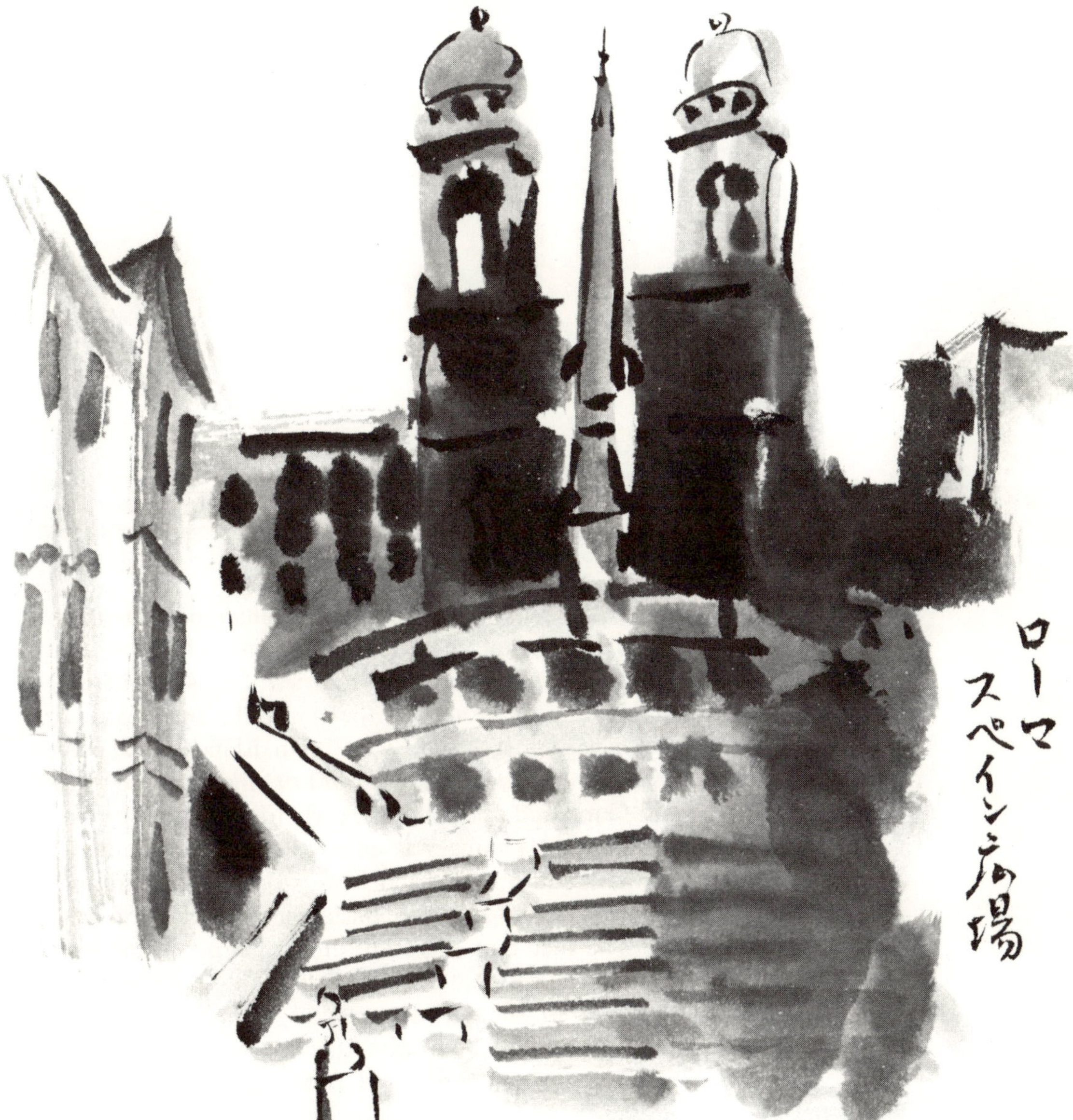
ローマ
スペイン広場

Suburbs of Odense, Denmark

The name Odense may not be a familiar one to some, but it is the birthplace of Hans Christian Andersen, and the tiny little house he lived in can still be seen there.

At first glance, the scenery looks just like our Hokkaido (the northernmost of the four main islands of Japan), and that is not without reason. For when the development of Hokkaido began in the early Meiji period (around 1870), Danish farming was adopted, with even buildings becoming Danish in style. It is no wonder that paintings of Hokkaido are, at times, mistaken for scenes of Denmark. The fact that there are numerous poplar trees in Hokkaido is also identical with Denmark.

The tree in the left foreground is painted in bold strokes, and is done so with the intention of adding a strong accent to the peaceful rural scene.

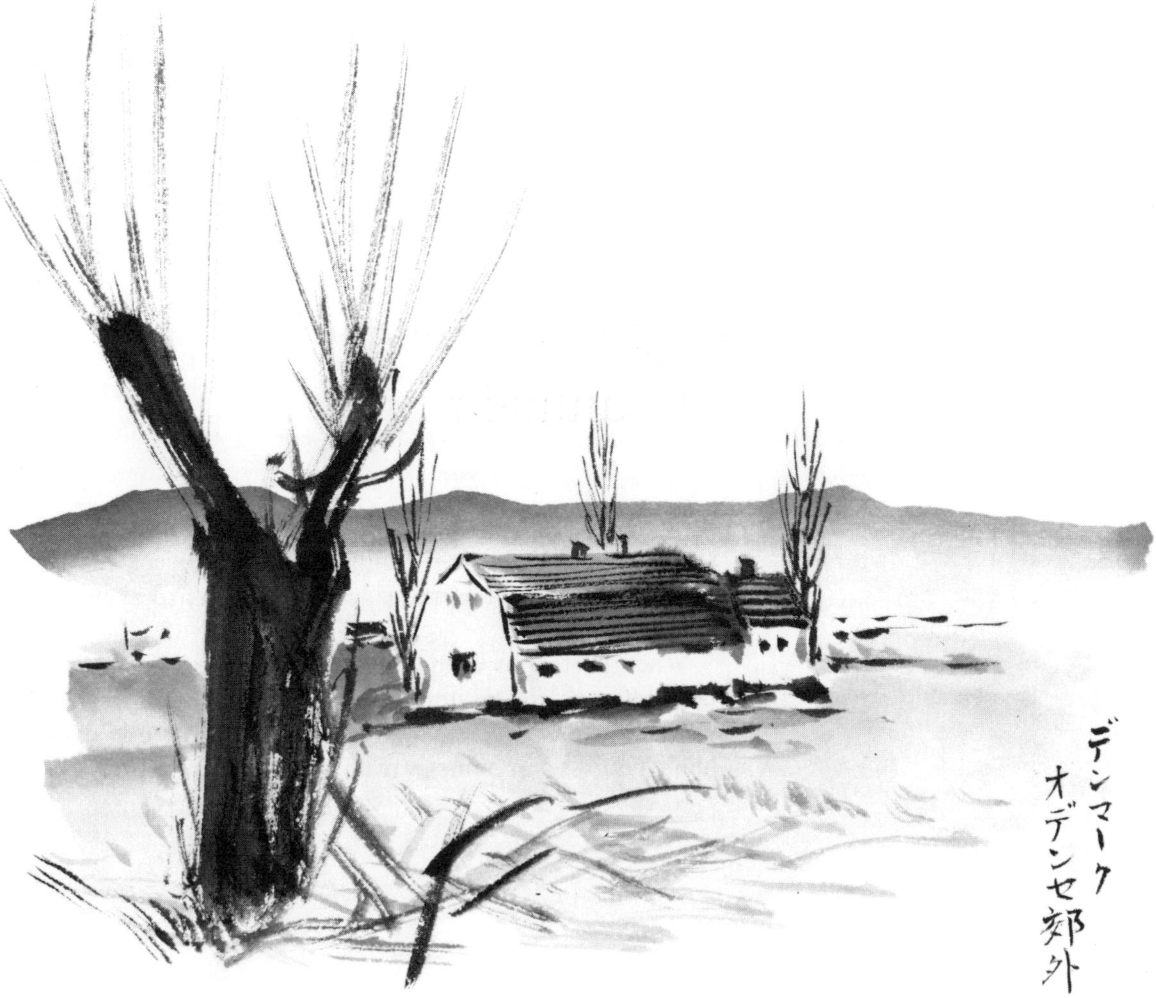

デンマーク
オデンセ郊外

The Banana Vender at Santarém

In a rural town in Portugal, I found a plump woman selling thin bananas. Coming by such subject matter, I inevitably bought some bananas and took to sketching her.

When sketching women in foreign countries, one must be careful not to be impolite or to offend them in doing so. To sketch them without saying a word or expressing one's courtesy in some way is out of the question.

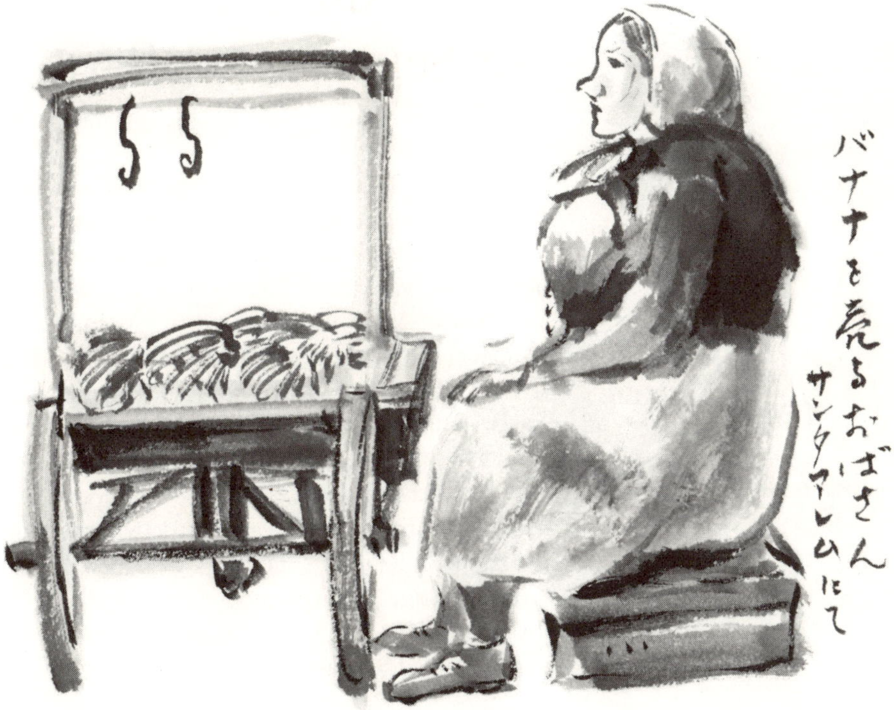
バナナを売るおばさん
サンタマレムにて

The Pont du Carrousel on the Seine River, Paris

This bridge is right by the Louvre. The two towers seen in the distance are those of Notre-Dame on the Île de la Cité, the main island in the Seine. The right hand edge of this painting is just about where you will find the École des Beaux-Arts. And behind it spreads out the Latin Quarter, the domain of students.

Beyond this whitish stone bridge extends ancient Paris, painted here in light ink, and from the bank on the left hang down the branches of the willow typical of those lining the Seine. An old boat goes down the river. This is certainly a landscape made to order for a Japanese brush with its lines and dots and flat areas.

The bridge was painted first, next the view in the distance, then the willow tree and bank, with the boat and water added last.

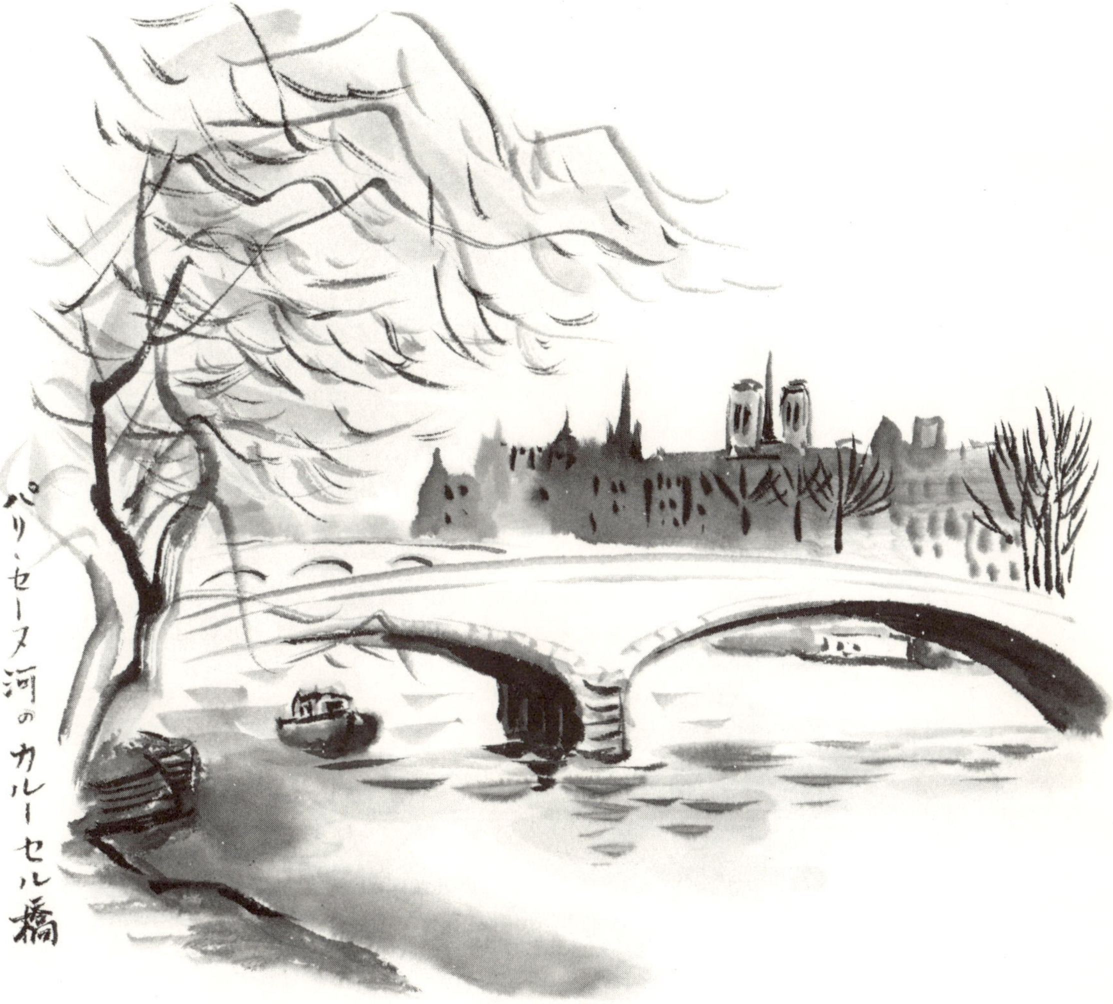
パリ、セーヌ河のカルーセル橋